OLIVER WIGHT

Class A Business Excellence
For

✓ Managing the Strategic Planning Process
✓ Managing and Leading People
✓ Driving Business Improvement
✓ Integrated Business Planning
✓ Managing Products and Services
✓ Managing Demand
✓ Managing the Supply Chain
✓ Managing Internal Supply
✓ Managing External Sourcing

The Oliver Wight Class A Checklist for Business Excellence

SIXTH EDITION

WILEY

John Wiley & Sons Inc.

Published by John Wiley & Sons, Inc., Hoboken, New Jersey.

Published simultaneously in Canada.

For general information on our other products and services please contact our Customer Care Department within the United States at (800) 762-2974, outside the United States at (317) 572-3993 or fax (317) 572-4002.

Wiley also publishes its books in a variety of electronic formats. Some content that appears in print may not be available in electronic books. For more information about Wiley products, visit our web site at www.wiley.com.

Library of Congress Cataloging-in-Publication Data:

The Oliver Wight Class A checklist for business excellence / Oliver Wight International, inc..—6th ed.
     p. cm.—(Oliver Wight manufacturing series)
  Rev. ed. of: Oliver Wight ABCD checklist for operational excellence. 5th ed. 2000.
Published simultaneously in Canada.
Includes bibliographical references.
ISBN-13 978-0-471-74106-0 (pbk.)
ISBN-10 0-471-74106-X (pbk.)
  1. Industrial productivity—Measurement. 2. Strategic planning. 3. Total quality management. 4. Manufacturing resource planning. 5. Production control. I. Wight, Oliver W. II. Oliver Wight International, inc. III. Oliver Wight ABCD checklist for operational excellence. IV. Series.
  HD56.25.O38 2005
  658.4'013—dc22

2005003952

Printed in the United States of America

10 9 8 7 6

CONTENTS

Additional clarification can be obtained from the Oliver Wight International website
(www.oliverwight.com) where a glossary can be found and the metrics to support
Performance Measures.

PREFACE

Welcome to the sixth edition of the *Oliver Wight Class A Checklist for Business Excellence,* which marks another major milestone on a journey started by Oliver Wight himself in the 1970s. His passion was to support companies seeking to be consistent winners by aspiring to excellence. This new Checklist is the comprehensive statement of excellence in business today.

It looks very different from our last version, with its scope widened to embrace every part of the business to be pursued for total excellence. Additionally, it now requires a demonstrated superior business performance for the coveted Class A award. However the major features remain and are unique.

- It is direct and practical. It does not follow the trend of setting theoretical business scoring criteria for you to "fill in." It sets out those business processes and practices that we see over and over at the heart of successful and excellent businesses.
- Its chapters align with core business processes and the enablers of those processes, covering the entire Business.
- It is aimed so that your people can see for themselves what "excellence" is and to appreciate what each individual has to do for the company to be excellent.
- Its scoring method allows you to visualize and measure progress towards excellence in every part of the Business.

The sixth edition offers the longest standing Excellence Award of international repute. It recognizes the efforts of your people and can be used with clients and customers to prove your efforts on their behalf.

The first checklist in 1977 was a simple list of 20 questions that a manager could answer to evaluate his business. It was the very first such list in the world and, consequently, the checklist concept became widely accepted. However, standards of excellence in business had started their own revolution. As a result, the list went from one page to a book, with each version building on the last. The questions were built from the accumulated experience of Oliver Wight's organization throughout the world and from the many people they worked with in thousands of companies.

The first checklist book was published in 1988 and was a major statement in defining excellent use of Manufacturing Resource Planning (MRPII) systems, continuous improvement processes, and the realization of sustainable processes. The fourth edition followed in 1993 and the fifth some seven years later in 2000. With each edition, the standard for excellence increased, and the scope of the business that was assessed widened as the world became ever more competitive and companies became larger and more international.

Throughout this adventure some things are unchanged:

- The Oliver Wight International organization continues to grow and set the standards in global business excellence.
- It operates throughout the world offering the same message in many languages for its multinational and multicultural client base.
- It holds to the same core belief that education and training at all levels of the company are the keys to achieving excellence.
- One other thing that remains unchanged is the role and purpose of this checklist.

Many have contributed to the know-how in this book, but we must recognize some people who have been major contributors.

- The book has been sponsored by the Oliver Wight International Board, and its development was led by Andrew Purton as its champion.
- The checklist architect, Lawrie Rumens, has brought his experience and expertise to the design forum to steer the journey to a superior Class A.
- The project leader, Lloyd Snowden, has spent so much time and energy driving very busy people and has delivered the book on time.
- Glyn Williams and Jon Minerich provided the global leadership.
- Each chapter had its own champion and sponsor supported by expert teams from the other regions. The chapters were led by Lawrie Rumens, Peter Hill, Andrew Purton, Les Brookes, Kevin Herbert, Liam Harrington, Ron Ireland, Lloyd Snowden, and Barry Linger.

    Chris Radford, Paul Archer, and Shirley Harrison also generously contributed.

- Last, where would we be without Jill Losik pulling it and us together in such an uncomplaining way?

So here is the sixth edition Checklist. It is no longer an MRP checklist or a manufacturing excellence standard. It is a standard of excellence for all businesses. We know that you will find it demanding, but then true excellence never did come easy. It will be rewarding as well. True excellence is the only way of consistently and reliably competing and winning in business. That's what Oliver Wight Class A is about, helping you to be in a position to win consistently in your business.

For those executives anxious to take up the challenge of raising their company's performances to heights of excellence, this Checklist will show them the way.

Walt Goddard
Chairman Emeritus,
Oliver Wight International, Inc.

INTRODUCTION

This updated sixth edition of the *Oliver Wight Class A Checklist for Business Excellence* follows the same style and approach to assessing excellence as before. Those of you familiar with the previous Checklist editions may notice that the sixth edition refers to "Business Excellence," with its broader scope, rather than the "Operational Excellence" of preceding editions.

The journey to business excellence is demanding, and this latest update takes into account the changes in business practices since the first printing in 2005. The changes in business expectations continue apace. Companies holding back from keeping up with the pack may be found wanting in the race to win in business.

WHAT IS DIFFERENT IN THIS UPDATED SIXTH EDITION?

We had to decide at the outset what few basic principles of excellence were important enough to be at the heart of the checklist. We have described these here in brief so that you can be familiar with the thinking before plunging into the detailed assessment. Clearly, we have only provided an overview of these principles in this section. However, you can find out more through Oliver Wight's global education programs.

Secondly, the checklist range has been extended from an operational focus to encompass all business processes and all business sectors. This will be no surprise since, across the world, manufacturing and service sectors are growing closer together in their characteristics. In many ways the new best practice manufacturing companies may be considered as service industries, but whose service is to sell products. Business differentiators have moved to managing products and services, managing the supply chain, managing the procurement of externally sourced items, and developing more effective relationships with employees, suppliers, customers, and consumers. All of these issues are now extensively covered alongside the more traditional foundation elements you would expect to find in this checklist. Further IT advances now permit dynamic business management where business performance, including financials, can be reviewed every day and where the installed agility permits the business to respond and move with market forces in days, not weeks or months.

THE CHAPTERS

The chapters are split into two groups. There are four priority chapters (Chapters 1–4) where we have brought together the processes and practices that are common to all businesses and that enable the whole business to be excellent.

• **Managing the Strategic Planning Process:** You have to be clear about business vision and strategy for your people to plan what has to be done to get there. This chapter will challenge your process for longer-term planning of the business. It will demand the setting of business priorities and clear communication when deploying your plans and your business excellence program throughout the business.

• **Managing and Leading People:** People are the ultimate differentiator as business gets more competitive and markets more demanding. This chapter will require you think through your business values and its organization for the tasks ahead; that you are clear about the company culture and behaviors that you need; and that you have active development programs designed to improve the competencies of your people for the new challenges ahead. It will also challenge your processes for Knowledge Management and your culture of leadership and teamwork.

• **Driving Business Improvement:** This articulates how you can assess the maturity of your business and its processes. It then challenges how you prioritize your Business Improvement Programs to the early gains areas that create a solid foundation for the future. You'll be challenged to walk before you try to run, and to give value to those everyday issues that are at the heart of excellence in business.

• **Integrated Business Planning:** Integrated Business Planning (IBP) is the holistic command and control process for all aspects of a business. It drives and directs revenue and earnings and overall business performance.

IBP is a process for both manufacturing and service sectors. At the core of IBP is Sales & Operations Planning (S&OP), originally developed by Oliver Wight as a vehicle to engage the senior management team in integrated management of the supply chain.

The IBP process is becoming the unique and increasingly de facto best practice approach to managing the gap between company strategic goals and everyday activity; it is the prime tool for keeping all parts of the company to a common agenda and set of priorities; and it manages the entire business through one set of numbers—dynamically tuned to the latest market situation that ensures timely actions to maintain management control of business performance. IBP provides long-term visibility and enables use of rigorous risk management tools to permit suitable contingency planning.

Chapters 5–9, the process chapters, address the prime business processes in most companies:

• **Managing Products and Services:** In every business sector, product life cycles are reducing. Portfolios require an increase in new products and services and a carefully planned phaseout of old. This chapter asks how well and how fast you set your product portfolio and manage products and services. It expects you to have a clear technology strategy to support this, including rapid/virtual prototyping to help increase the speed to market. It challenges your practices for delivering sales and profit to your business through an increased number of successful launches of products and services into your market. It includes expectations of the latest practices in the program management of large complex projects, and computer-aided risk management and decision making to anticipate and avoid adverse consequences.

• **Managing Demand:** Greater understanding of customer needs and of what is happening in your marketplace leads directly to increased predictability in the short-, medium-, and long-term needs of your business. It enables better planning of your position in the marketplace, and order-winning plans that are more successful. This chapter challenges how close you are to real demand knowledge, how well you create and plan demand, and how professionally you control supply and demand in the very short term through sales activity driving a demand-led supply chain.

• **Managing the Supply Chain:** As your marketplace becomes ever more global, the increasing challenge to business is how to deliver the product and service to the point of use. This chapter challenges how well you understand your extended supply chain both strategically and operationally through supply network planning and optimization techniques to achieve best customer service and business performance.

- **Managing Internal Supply:** While business focus is moving to the extended supply chain, excellence in the core supply activities remains vital to live up to the promises and wishes of customers and consumers, and to meet the challenge of global cost competition. This chapter challenges whether your operations that make and deliver goods and services understand what is excellent today and how quickly they must respond to changes and the demand of the marketplace.

- **Managing External Sourcing:** The increase in products and services and the wider market present new challenges to our make/buy decision process at product, component, and material levels. They also impact the sourcing strategies that follow those decisions. Technology offers new procurement approaches that have major potential for saving, and this has significantly advanced the use of Total Cost of Ownership in critical decision making. This chapter sets new standards for assessing excellence in your procurement processes and in the planning and coordination of movement of goods into your supply chain.

MEASURES

Prime performance measures are included at the end of each chapter of this Checklist, but we have not included in the book the detailed recommended measures. In a fast-moving world, we wanted to be able to update and add freely to these. So you will find them openly available on our website at *www.oliverwight.com*, along with a new glossary that is designed to take away the confusion of any new terminology. You will find this approach more relevant to your business needs.

RECOGNITION OF EXCELLENCE

The scoring system uses the five-point scale, and a way of recognizing your steps toward excellence. We are mindful that against a broader and higher standard it will take you longer from the same starting point to achieve full Class A Business Excellence in practices and performance than the previous checklists. As you start this journey to excellence, while you may be focusing on a solution to the latest business needs, we recommend that you set a total excellence program with incremental prioritized projects and initiatives, each giving you business gains in a relatively short timescale while taking you a step further toward your longer goals. Our recognition of your success will come in three forms:

- **Oliver Wight Class A:** The full Class A award when an entire business meets the requirements of all chapters of this checklist.
- **Oliver Wight Business Unit Class A Accreditation:** To recognize the achievements of a stand-alone business within a larger multiunit business that meets all the requirements of its appropriate chapters.
- **Oliver Wight Class A Milestone Award:** To recognize predetermined projects and milestones in your business improvement program that have delivered their planned business gains on the journey to Class A Business Excellences. There is an award for each milestone you achieve.

The demands on a successful business are racing ahead, and without an aggressive excellence program, you will fall behind your competition. Your Business Improvement Program must be structured and targeted to deliver rewards for your customers and your owners and be the basis for winning consistently in business.

FOUNDATION

As each day passes, companies in every sector of business get faster, smarter, and more innovative. In producing this latest version of our Checklist of Business Excellence, we have set a new Class A standard of excellence and established the basic principles that are important for a company to achieve outstanding performance today. This section sets out those foundations and documents the main assumptions we have made about practices and processes in excellent companies.

ACHIEVING EXCELLENCE

Our first assumption is that we are all in business to win. Excellent companies win consistently and win more than their competition. They set the standards in their chosen markets and serve their customers better than the competition. They outperform the competition sufficiently to differentiate. There is no point in any excellence program if it is not consistent with what your customer wants.

Our second assumption is that such companies also will outperform in delivering what their owners, the shareholders, want in cash flow, return on assets, and growth.

Lastly, all the other company stakeholders also have to be satisfied, especially the community and its environment and, of course, the employees who are increasingly the biggest differentiator that any company can have.

EXCELLENT PERFORMANCE

Each chapter captures the vast knowledge and experience of Oliver Wight Associates around the world, and our thousands of clients, in setting out the practices and processes that are understood to represent excellence today. This is a minimum standard for an excellent company. You may be fortunate that your business sits in a sector that is relatively undemanding, but be assured that the demands of excellence will come and will come faster than you may expect. Alternatively, you may find that you are in a very demanding sector and that you need to be in advance of these standards to win. This may be so, but understand that the foundations of excellence are the same for every company in every sector, and they are the entry qualification to any higher performance. We are setting our minimum standard as the practical foundation for wherever this exciting world takes us next.

The Oliver Wight 6th Edition Checklist provides a process to define excellence for your company. This definition will drive the targets and goals of the company. The process tells your company enough about itself and its market to put numbers on the targets and goals. An Excellence company exhibits "upper-quartile" performance in its sector. We do not see this as a complex concept nor as a demand on you that leads to eternal statistical debate. Put simply, you know what being ahead of the game means for you, and you can demonstrate that your balanced performance to all your stakeholders puts you in the upper quartile of companies in your sector or marketplace. You know how you will maintain that winning position. You will be challenged on this in the chapter "Managing the Strategic Planning Process."

THE JOURNEY TO EXCELLENCE

For more detail of the journey to excellence you might want to read the companion volume to the Checklist, *Achieving Class A Business Excellence: An Executive's Perspective* (2008).

The journey to excellence is tough and uncompromising. It is never ending and is applied to every part and every process in the company. For such a journey to be sustained it must continually deliver results and gains for all its stakeholders. The journey is a series of bite-sized projects with short timescales. These build into a longer business improvement program that assures success now and in the future. Improvement activity must be prioritized to the current needs of stakeholders while delivering the firm foundations for future advanced work. As in building a house, we risk everything if we are not sure that the right foundations are firmly in place before we start the walls, and that they too are right before starting the roof and on to the finishing processes.

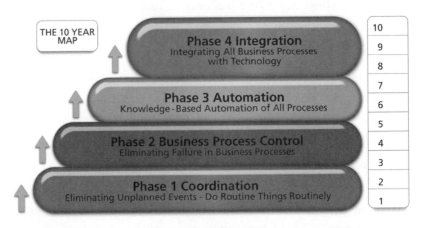

Figure I.1: The Oliver Wight Business Maturity Map Phases

The Oliver Wight Business Maturity Map (see Figure I.1) enables you to understand the maturity of your business, and by derivation, the focus for your business improvement program to deliver real gains. This is addressed in the Oliver Wight education, which is arranged both publicly and privately in all parts of the world.

We must stress that excellence is not doing what we do today better. It means adopting new processes and culture to a different, more effective, and dynamic paradigm.

You must address the root causes of firefighting or reactive (even knee-jerk) management in your business. These create plan imbalances. Unplanned events may be driven from the marketplace because your customers require more than your standard processes can deliver, or they may arise from your own in-house indiscipline in the way you work, and your behaviors as a total team. Left unresolved, firefighting drains management time and energy in solving the same issues over and over. It prevents gains from problem-solving and team-based initiatives being sustained. Tackling the root causes behind being event-driven constitutes Phase 1 of your journey toward excellence. (See Phase 1 in Figure I.1.) With the foundation of a well-planned and coordinated business in place, you are ready for the next step.

Your priority business need may be to accelerate your processes, make them more agile, and maybe absolutely eliminate the root causes of failure in them. By doing so, you will be capturing the knowledge and experience of your people at all levels of the company into its processes and procedures so that it is not lost when people move on. Projects that eliminate the root causes of failures and embed knowledge in your company processes form Phase 2 of your journey toward excellence. This checklist is benchmarked and expects that processes and behaviors of a Class A company will be in the top half of this Phase 2 maturity.

Phase 2 enables a step change in productivity and effectiveness is sought by implanting this accumulated knowledge of the business into its systems and machines. Increasingly those systems become more intelligent and require less and less human intervention in decision making. People play a more vital role at this time as knowledge workers, focusing on the integrity and management of sophisticated processes and leading innovation to even higher performance. This phase may well increase the number of computer-controlled machines in your operations and office processes. It does involve the latest IT to leverage knowledge management and near real-time communication. It is about your confidence that those systems will make the right decisions in all circumstances.

Phases 3 and 4 are not yet included in this checklist, however, the standards we have included ensure that you will be well prepared for this activity.

IMPROVING THE EARLY PHASES

Most of us will be in businesses predominantly in the first two phases.

How much of your working time is spent dealing with unplanned events, and what can you do about it? The Oliver Wight Jigsaw Puzzle (see Figure I.2) helps us to understand this more.

The analogy here is simple. When we do a jigsaw puzzle at home, we tend to look for the corner pieces first because they are easy to find, quick to put in place, and they give foundation and structure to everything else. Of course we leave the work on the blue sky to the end when we have more context to work with. So if you want to eliminate unplanned events from your business, as in Phase 1, then the four most rewarding actions are likely to come from addressing the jigsaw puzzle corner pieces.

1. Ensuring that people undertake their work consistently, using the approved processes that are always up to date. Without this standardization culture, improved processes will be followed no better than the old. You will be challenged on this issue in the "Managing and Leading People" chapter.

Figure I.2: The Oliver Wight Jigsaw Puzzle

2. Ensuring that your people own, and are responsible for, the work that they do and the improvement of the processes they use. They will also own their workplace, its maintenance, and any tools, machines, or systems that they use every day. You will be challenged on this in the "Driving Business Improvement" chapter.

3. Having one clear set of priorities and one set of numbers that are acknowledged and used throughout the business. There must be one clear agenda from the top to the bottom of the company and across all its processes and functions. The Oliver Wight Integrated Business Planning process tackles this issue, and you will be challenged on this in the "Integrated Business Planning" chapter.

4. Having robust planning processes that support the company game plan, which is realistic and which is followed and routinely fulfilled throughout the business. You will be challenged on this in the relevant process chapters.

Getting these cornerstones firmly in place will assure you that Phase 1 of the maturity map is sound enough to build Phase 2 activities. Phase 2 activities accelerate the processes in the company and make them failure free, more automated, and at near real-time speeds through knowledge-based systems. They are typified by the jigsaw edge pieces and are detailed in the challenges posed in the "Driving Business Improvement" chapter.

THE INTEGRATED BUSINESS MODEL

The Oliver Wight Integrated Business Model is shown in its simple form in Figure I.3. It is powered by Integrated Business Planning; supported by the core operational processes for Product, Demand, Supply Management, and External Sourcing; and within a strategic context, enabled by business improvement techniques and people and behavioral dynamics.

The chapter structure in the checklist describes all the elements of this Integrated Business Model.

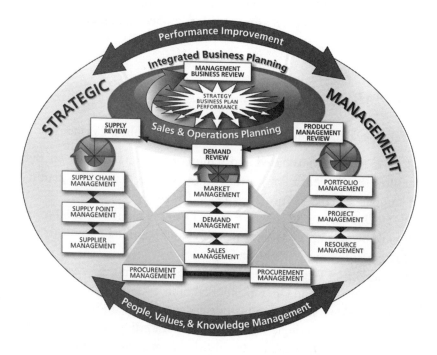

Figure I.3: The Oliver Wight Integrated Business Model

THE IMPORTANCE OF PEOPLE

Last, we must return to the subject of your people. To be more effective and productive you must move knowledge from your people into the systems of the company. As productivity increases, you have the opportunity to grow the company significantly. As processes become more sophisticated and higher performing, your people become knowledge workers who are crucially important to the company and its performance. You will be challenged to manage processes rather than functional silos; those processes will need people to work together in self-managed teams where disciplines and functions are mixed together to run the business and your people will be faced with ever more complex tools and systems through which the business is run. We set out the challenge on people in the "Managing and Leading People" chapter. It asks how they are valued, how they are led, how they are developed, how they find out what is going on in the business, and most important of all, how their successes are recognized across the company. People are your biggest business differentiator now and will be more so as your excellence program matures. Treasure, develop, and educate them. They are the future.

SUMMARY

Our Checklist is founded on clear and well-established principles:

1. It is performance based and requires you to have a process that identifies the challenge for you to win in your sector and to quantify what upper-quartile performance means for you.

2. The journey to excellence for any business requires a solid foundation of ownership, consistent working, and planning upon which to build high-gain improvement activity.

3. The Oliver Wight Integrated Business Planning process, which evolved from Sales and Operational Planning, is the standard for keeping a business on a single agenda of priorities, actions, and performance and is measured by a single set of figures. The monthly formal process is reinforced by dynamic day-to-day holistic management enabled by the latest IT infrastructure.

4. Robust planning and execution processes that are both increasing in velocity are needed to manage the business.

HOW TO USE THE CHECKLIST

THE OLIVER WIGHT CLASS A CHECKLIST

This is by far the longest running excellence checklist available to you that is regularly updated with latest practices and process knowledge, as evidenced by this update. It is not a theoretical or academic model but is the accumulated knowledge and experience of Oliver Wight Associates across the world and their clients in thousands of companies.

- It is a real benchmark of excellence today, which must be used to raise awareness of what is possible and to challenge the status quo.
- It establishes the gaps in every part of the business between your status today and where you would need to be to increase competitiveness—or at worst, to catch up. It enables you to establish a prioritized agenda for your journey to a defined Class A standard of excellence.
- It provides a mechanism to cascade ownership for change and for achieving excellence to those actually engaged on performing work every day, encouraging them to be a part of the assessment and sharing ownership of the results.
- It is a vehicle to coordinate and integrate multiple actions across all business processes in a consistent approach to excellence in a holistic manner.
- It provides an agenda with clear recognition of achievements and provides public and global recognition.
- It is the best way of engaging the entire workforce, top-down and bottom-up, in an ongoing total excellence program that delivers real and sustained business gains.

CHECKLIST STRUCTURE

Within each chapter there are typically ten main subjects, most of which have two definitions of excellence. It is the scoring of each definition that determines your overall score for the chapter and whether you have reached Class A Business Excellence standards in this business process.

To help you determine this score, each definition is further divided into (typically) five topics, each with its own detailed description.

There is an opportunity to score each of these descriptions to help you to the right score for the definition and to see in greater depth your performance gaps. However, these detailed scores are not directly used in scoring a chapter and a total business. Only the definition scores count.

USING THE CHECKLIST

The checklist is a practical assessment tool that is used for original gap analysis, for prioritization of activity and discrete improvement projects, and for ongoing review of progress of the journey toward Total Business Excellence.

Those conducting the assessment must be educated and knowledgeable about best practices in business in order to interpret the definitions and descriptions for the business being assessed. It is easy to award unreasonably high or low scores when not intimately familiar with excellence and best-practice standards generally held in the subject and without close knowledge of the intent behind the definition and its descriptions.

To get a balanced view of the complete process or the total business it is also important to understand the integrated nature of the checklist and the interrelationships between the priority and the process chapters. As a result of this the checklist cannot be addressed chapter by chapter. Hence it utilizes milestones to achieve desired goals.

The prioritization of improvement projects requires a practical and working knowledge of the Oliver Wight Business Maturity Map to identify the appropriate early projects (milestones) to give quick gains while also laying the foundation for the total excellence journey.

For all of these reasons an independently facilitated approach to the initial diagnostic and ongoing assessment of your business is strongly recommended. The summarized sequence of events in a program of work look like this:

- Clearly identify and agree the scope of the Checklist that applies to your business.
- Through an Oliver Wight structured diagnostic assessment, understand the gaps and opportunities.
- Set a manageable program of excellence activity (milestone) through the whole business that allows the total business to advance, together with clear deliverables that benefit the business stakeholders.
- Establish at the outset the work and deliverables that will qualify for the unique Oliver Wight Class A Milestone Award for each substantial business improvement achieved.
- Create a meaningful plan that can be resourced and afforded for the steps in the entire journey to Oliver Wight Class A Business Excellence.

SCORING AND RECOGNITION

The scoring system is based on a scale of 0 to 5, in 0.5 increments only. (Finer increments would suggest a precision that does not exist!) Oliver Wight are the scorers of reference, but internal scoring should be consensus based. This means that if a group of managers score the same definition, say, 2.0, 3.5, and 4, then the same group should discuss the rationale in each case to enhance their understanding and to avoid over- or underscoring.

The scores are defined as:

- **Score 0 (Not Doing):** Practices are required for this business, but they do not exist at present.
- **Score 1 (Poor):** Practices exist, but they have not been developed to contribute to the business and its improvement.
- **Score 2 (Fair):** Practices have been developed in isolation from the rest of the business. They have delivered benefit but are not integrated or formalized into the business processes.
- **Score 3 (Good):** Practices are formalized and their checklist definitions are being satisfied; however, they have not yet been subjected to a systematic application of continuous improvement techniques.

- **Score 4 (Very Good):** Practices are fully integrated into the company's business processes, and all checklist definitions and description characteristics are routinely achieved, and continuous improvement demonstrated.
- **Score 5 (Excellent):** Practices are excellent and fully effective in the company. They successfully and sustainably deliver its business goals and the checklist defined minimum standard or upper-quartile performance.

An average score of 4.5 is required for all definitions in the agreed scope for Business Excellence Class A recognition. However, before this can be awarded, the business performance measures for each chapter must also be fully satisfied and sustained for at least three consecutive months, with only one failure in six months permitted.

RECOGNITION

This excellence standard will be more demanding (and rewarding), and it may require a longer period of improvement. Pursuit of Class A will require a business improvement program with targeted fast-track projects and milestones. Each fast-track project will give significant business benefits in a short time. The milestones then complete the steps towards Class A and also serve as major points for recognition. Recognition of agreed business deliverables along the journey will sustain the longer drive for business excellence. Achievement of these agreed milestones and their deliverables will be rewarded with an Oliver Wight Class A Milestone Award, and will mark significant progress to Oliver Wight Class A Business Excellence. Our experience with clients is that each project and milestone program within the business improvement program will offer significant and sustainable benefits.

Recognition can be only be provided by the Oliver Wight organization, and will be at three levels:

- **Oliver Wight Class A Milestone Award:** Derived from the business diagnostic and business strategic priorities, each recognizable milestone will be a significant step forward for the business and will demonstrate measurable benefits to the company and its stakeholders. Each Milestone is likely to be of six to 12 months in duration, but some may overlap or be addressed in parallel.

- **Oliver Wight Business Unit Class A Accreditation:** This recognizes the effort and achievement of a stand-alone business unit within a larger business that achieves the Class A requirements for all of its agreed scope.
- **Oliver Wight Class A:** This is the only full Class A certification, and it is only awarded to a fully integrated business.

IMPLEMENTATION

Each company will develop its own approach to its business improvement program. The business need is the overriding priority for any excellence program, and this guarantees relevance to people at all levels of the business. This characterization will be displayed most in determining the priorities of the milestone steps toward business excellence and the consequent resource allocations across the company. It is expected that a Class A implementation will include the following steps:

- Agreement of the scope of the intended Class A business improvement program.
- Initial diagnostic against the full checklist scope to identify excellence gaps and to establish and quantify the competing opportunities for improvement.
- Prioritization of activity to the company strategic goals and the agreement of a series of milestones and their identified projects. Each milestone project will be significant and will be goal driven with clear performance targets and measures.
- Milestone project implementation using the education-led Oliver Wight Proven Path Process and full checklist assessment, used to develop the scoped and phased milestones program to establish and manage the change program.
- Milestone achievement recognition based on checklist assessment and performance for the scope of the project, including the priority chapters.
- And for Class A Business Excellence, full assessment against all nine chapters of the checklist.
- Ongoing annual assessment to identify new challenges and further relevant best practices as well as to assure that the Class A standard is being sustained.

SUMMARY

An excellence program is vital for every company to beat its rivals and enable growth in its marketplace. Only the excellent companies will consistently win in business. The required standard of excellence increases every day as customers expect more value—and shareholders expect more return.

An excellence program will unite your people and provide a common set of goals that engages them all. It is exciting and energizing for them and for your customers and suppliers. It is guaranteed to achieve a pace of change that cannot be sustained by the top team alone.

1
MANAGING THE STRATEGIC PLANNING PROCESS

PURPOSE

To establish and manage the process for setting vision, strategy, and direction in order to be an upper-quartile company. To ensure that this is reflected in all plans, projects, and actions throughout the company.

Chapter Content

Understanding and Analyzing the Internal and External Environment
Business Mission, Vision, and Values
Strategic Planning
Supporting Process and Function Strategies
Strategy Development
Business Planning and Annualized Plans
Evaluation and Control
Business Strategy Management Process
Risk Management
Performance Measures
Behavioral Characteristics

UNDERSTANDING AND ANALYZING THE INTERNAL AND EXTERNAL ENVIRONMENT

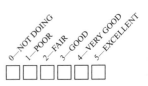

1. A process exists to collect relevant information internally and externally to understand the company, its products and services, its market place, and the competition.

a. <u>Company Capability</u>

The company has a process to understand the capability of all its business processes to identify the strengths and weaknesses of its offer to the market place.

b. <u>Industry Position</u>

The company actively seeks information and input from inside and outside its sector to identify best practices and excellent performance in all its processes and at all company levels. It can show its industry position and measure that it performs at least as an upper-quartile company in its sector.

c. <u>Stakeholder Goals</u>

The major stakeholders in the company are identified and their short-, medium-, and long-term goals are understood. The company has a balanced view of goals and targets.

d. <u>Market Analysis</u>

Sufficient investigation and analysis is carried out to understand the market in which the company operates, its competitors' activity, and the value of its opportunities. This may include trends in geographic focus, consumer and customer demands, economic trends, and national and international policies and regulations, and so on.

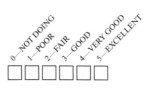

e. <u>Products and Services Portfolio</u>

All parts of the products and services portfolio are examined to ensure the voices of the consumer and customer are understood and life-cycle trends are identified. The potential of competitor actions, technology discontinuities, breakthroughs in technology, and the market place have been assessed.

2. This information is analyzed using appropriate tools to identify and prioritize opportunities and challenges for the success of the business model.

a. <u>Information Analysis</u>

Information is analyzed to form a picture in words and figures of potential futures for the strategic plan horizon. Potential breakthrough areas for technical and nontechnical innovation are sought and identified for the company to differentiate from its competitors.

b. <u>Analytical Tools</u>

A comprehensive use of analytical tools is made to identify business trends and opportunities and to understand how the company responds to current and future consumer needs.

c. <u>Capability Diagnostic</u>

A diagnostic is prepared and agreed showing the capability of the company in all its processes and its adequacies or limitations for the future.

d. <u>Opportunities</u>

The challenges and opportunities for the company from inside the company and from its external environment over the strategic plan horizon are understood and documented.

e. <u>Prioritization</u>

Opportunities to meet the business strategy are prioritized using established filter criteria, and the potential risk to the business from each opportunity is understood.

BUSINESS MISSION, VISION, AND VALUES

3. Mission and vision statements exist, representing the balanced views of the company (or business unit) and its stakeholders.

a. <u>Top Down Team-Based</u>

The company mission, vision, and strategy are for a suitable long-term horizon appropriate to the business. They are initiated and agreed by the chief executive officer and the company leadership team, and other functional heads and key players, and they are shared and supported by the entire organization.

b. <u>The Mission Statement</u>

The mission statement is a clear and concise statement of the company's strategic intent. It summarizes the main purpose of the business or business unit and the value that its products and services bring to customers, consumers, and society.

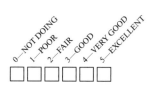

c. The Vision Statement

The vision statement is inspiring and memorable, and summarizes concisely what the company wants to become in its market place and community.

d. The Expanded Vision Statement

The Expanded Vision statement paints a picture in words and overview figures to show employees, customers, suppliers, and shareholders what the company plans to become in the medium and long term. It is sufficient for them to relate their actions and behaviors and their sense of values. It is long term enough to be independent of business cycles.

4. The company values shape the business strategies and supporting plans. They are captured in a values statement and are lived throughout the company.

a. Ownership

The company values are owned by the chief executive officer and the leadership team and are formally documented in a values statement that is discussed and agreed with all the company stakeholders.

b. The Values Statement

The values statement sets out the guiding principles and ethics by which the company will be known. It embodies how the company wishes to be perceived by all its stakeholders and is the prime driver for setting the culture of the business.

c. Communication

The company values are formally presented to everyone in the company, and this process is used to create excitement and purpose and to stimulate behavior change.

d. Living the Values

The company values are reviewed regularly and are used on an everyday basis to challenge the behaviors and culture of everyone in the company and to inspire all to improve continuously.

STRATEGIC PLANNING

5. A business strategic plan exists to support the mission and vision statement that is focused on strategic business objectives. It enables the alignment of all company processes and functional plans and the deployment of a hierarchy of measures.

a. Value Proposition

The strategic plan contains clear direction on the company value proposition (strategic values or value discipline), outlining how the company will differentiate as an upper-quartile performer in its chosen markets.

b. The Strategic Plan and Competing Priorities

The plan sets out for the medium and long term, the policies, goals, financial strategy, actions, and milestones for the company to attain its vision and firmly sets out the company's Strategic Business Objectives. Its competing initiatives and ambitions are prioritized against a timeline. It is long term enough to be independent of business cycles.

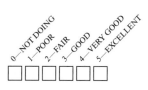

c. Strategic Business Objectives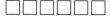

The goals for the company are clearly stated in quantifiable Strategic Business Objectives, which are formally agreed and documented and are each owned by a member of the leadership team. The Strategic Business Objectives are the driving force for change throughout the organization. It drives the hierarchy of goals and objectives in all separate or integrated units of the business.

d. Validity and Affordability

The strategic plan has sufficient operational analysis and plans to ensure that it is valid and achievable and contains sufficient financial analysis to ensure that it is viable and can be funded.

e. Risk Analysis

The main risks are formally identified and documented, and actions to reduce risks and risk contingency plans are identified.

f. Organization Roles

The role of every part of the present and future organization and its planned achievement is defined. The prime measures in the hierarchy of measures are derived from the Strategic Business Objectives, and are identified, agreed, and owned by a member of the leadership team.

6. **The assumptions generated through all parts of the strategic planning process are captured and formally documented. They are revalidated as additional information becomes available and are regularly reviewed and monitored.**

a. <u>Documentation of Assumptions</u>

The assumptions made in the construction and the agreement of the strategic plan are identified and are formally documented and communicated. Ownership of assumptions exists throughout the organization.

b. <u>Validity</u>

The assumptions are sufficiently tested to ensure that they are valid and are confirmed and applied throughout the business. Wherever possible, they are measured by their owners so that early warning of change is given.

c. <u>Monitoring and Reporting</u>

Key assumptions are monitored and reported through the formal Integrated Business Planning process on a regular basis.

SUPPORTING PROCESS AND FUNCTION STRATEGIES

7. The business strategic plan is appropriately supported by strategies for the core processes of the business that collectively deliver the company goals.

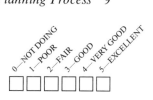

a. Market Strategy

There is a market analysis and planning process culminating in a market strategy to meet the growth and profitability aspirations of the business policies and plans covering the market sectors to be pursued. It also covers direction about the geography of the business and its planned channels and routes to market. The market strategy drives the company demand management processes and reviews.

b. Product and Services Strategy

There is clear analysis and direction on the products and services the company chooses to sell to meet its business aspirations, culminating in a product and services strategy. It includes direction for each product family or brand, its targeted consumers and customers, geographies, and the expected trends in product life cycles. It may include the company technology strategy and will drive the company product management processes and reviews and require a critical mass of identified core competencies.

c. Financial Strategy

There is a financial strategy for the business that sets out how the strategic plan will be viably funded and supported. It shows how the shareholder value and returns will be protected and grown. It defines the potential sources of funds and how those funds will be used. It will outline how the provision and use of financial information will be developed to promote and support advances in the business.

d. Operations Strategy

There is an operations strategy that defines how the company processes will be developed to meet future service and costs targets and to introduce new products and services most effectively. It reflects the company's competitive priorities. It covers processes from suppliers to consumers and from customer orders to invoicing, and includes a capital investment strategy that drives the company's make/buy policies. The strategy defines the role and focus of each operating unit and drives the company supply management processes and reviews.

8. Detailed strategies for key supporting functions are also derived from the business strategic plan and should, at minimum, include human resources (HR), information technology (IT), and any other process enabler important to the business.

a. HR Strategy

The company is committed to excellence, and its values are demonstrated at all levels. The role of people as a major differentiator is understood, and a strategy and plan exists to focus the acquisition, development, recognition, and motivation of the skills and competencies that are key to its future success. It includes practical succession planning to cover potential gaps in key positions and competencies.

b. IT Strategy

The strategic plan is supported by an IT strategy that sets out the architecture and framework for systems and communication tools for the future. The strategy prioritizes planned investment in IT (as part of the company capital investment strategy) to support the business processes and its strategic initiatives and determines how it will be managed. The need to educate as well as train users and managers in the processes and required behaviors to secure the potential business gains from investments is recognized.

c. Data Strategy

A data strategy exists to define the static and dynamic information needs of the business and its partners and how they will be satisfied. Its implementation is owned by the leadership team. Data quality and integrity is understood as a foundation requirement and discipline for excellence and is measured throughout the organization.

STRATEGY DEPLOYMENT

9. The competing priorities of the business and its performance goals are resolved to determine the priority of strategic projects and their skill and capability requirements. Projects are justified by demonstrating a compelling need and case for change.

a. Performance and Capability Gap Analysis

The gap between current capability and future plans and needs is understood, and the benefits and time phasing of planned changes is quantified.

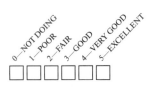

b. <u>Business-Based Competitive Priorities</u>

Proposed initiatives that compete with each other for attention are assessed using established and agreed criteria and are prioritized to the overall business needs during the lifetime of the strategic plan.

c. <u>Project Approval</u>

Each planned project is formally approved before work commences, and the need and case for change is proved with detailed business benefits and resource implications. Approved projects are held in a company-wide project master plan with agreed planned start and completion times, identified interdependencies, and ownership and sponsorship within the leadership team.

d. <u>Skill Competence Analysis</u>

The skill and competence base of the company is formally assessed against the strategic plan. Its strengths and weaknesses against timelines are understood, a gap analysis is conducted, and improvements are planned. Gap-closure actions are assigned and drive the education, training, selection, and succession plans for the business.

10. Strategic plans are converted into goals at every level of the business with detailed and prioritized action and resource plans. They are cascaded and explained to all people, demonstrating the need and plan for change.

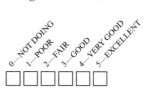

a. Communication Process and Listening

The vision for the business is widely communicated in a succinct, consistent, and repeatable way with opportunity for builds and feedback, and strategic goals and plans are cascaded to working levels with ownership and sponsorship.

b. Deployment of Goals and Targets

The performance targets required to fulfill the business strategy and the goals outlined in approved and planned improvement projects are represented as goals and targets at all levels of the business. Accountabilities are assigned and are part of the appraisal process.

c. Detailed Project Plans

Approved projects have detailed plans for goal achievement with supporting resource and capability plans to develop and allocate the appropriate skills and competencies.

d. People Development Plans

Plans are prepared and actioned to prepare people for the change program and projects. People with talent, development potential, and leadership skills are identified, and personal development plans are instituted.

e. Measures and Reviews

Formal processes and tools are used to manage, review, and measure projects and goals at all levels. Management by exception is commonplace and proactive corrective action plans are communicated.

BUSINESS PLANNING AND ANNUALIZED PLANS

11. The early years of the strategy are defined in the business plan and are the foundation of the company's annualized plans. They are used throughout the company for individual and team goal setting.

a. Business Plan (Multiyear Plan)

The plan for implementation of the early years of the business strategy is contained in the top level business plan covering at least two years. The business plan is the foundation of all other plans and projects over the business plan horizon.

b. Annual Plan (or Budget)

The annual plan (or budget) shows in depth an integrated view of how the business strategy and plan will be met, with owned targets and goals to achieve that reach down to every individual or team.

c. Affordable

The resource requirement of the business plan and annual plan (or budget) is regularly reviewed, and their affordability is formally checked to ensure validity.

d. Integrated Business Planning

The business plan and the annual plan (or budget) are prime references for the monthly Integrated Business Planning process.

12. The business plan is the main driver of the company annual plan (or budget), management control, and gap-closing activity.

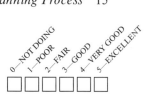

a. <u>Alignment to Strategy</u>

The annual plan (or budget) is driven top down from the business strategy and bottom up from the company Integrated Business Planning processes and is in alignment with the business plan.

b. <u>Budget Information</u>

Information from the Integrated Business Planning process is directly used to compile the annual plan/budget.

c. <u>Suite of Measures</u>

A balanced suite of measures is in place at the top of the company, showing how well the interests of all the stakeholders are managed. This suite is at the head of an integrated hierarchy of measures for the whole business that are used to monitor progress and drive action.

d. <u>Assumption Management</u>

The assumptions behind the strategic plan, the business plan, and the annual plan (or budget) is aligned, formally recognized, and documented. They are regularly monitored and reviewed, and plans and assumptions are updated as required. Assumptions are carried forward into the company Integrated Business Planning process.

EVALUATION AND CONTROL

13. Formal and informal periodic reviews are held to confirm the alignment of forward strategies at all company levels and between processes and specialist functions.

a. Diagnostic Review

On an annual basis, a formal diagnostic review of strategy deployment is undertaken. This will usually be a complete review of one sample strategic business objective to gauge the depth of its understanding throughout the business and the alignment of all business processes to achieve its goals.

b. Reflection

At least twice per year, the diagnostic is supported by an informal reflection of the strategic plan where a few key individuals come together to assess mutually the health and understanding of a particular Strategic Business Objective.

c. Resource Allocation

Strategic initiatives are included in the reporting and resource allocations in the Integrated Business Planning process.

14. Results are regularly reviewed to ensure that the deployment and implementation of strategy delivers the company plans.

a. Project Organization

A project organization exists that embraces all strategic initiatives. It gives visibility of their progress and enables balanced cross-functional priorities and resource allocation.

b. Project Reviews

Project plans are regularly reviewed by line managers and sponsors from the leadership team, and decisions are made to keep them on course for success.

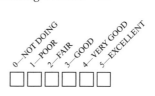

c. <u>Payback</u>

Projected and actual business gains are measured and project-based assumptions are reviewed to ensure that a project remains viable and worthy of completion.

d. <u>Communication</u>

Project launch, progress, and completion are widely communicated to recognize the efforts of those involved and to create an ongoing excitement and appetite for change throughout the workforce and its partner resources.

BUSINESS STRATEGY MANAGEMENT PROCESS

15. A dynamic process exists to ensure that the impact of decisions and events on the business strategy and plan are visible, understood, and agreed.

a. <u>Integrated Business Planning</u>

The company is managed through an Integrated Business Planning process, which reviews the activity and forward plans for all company processes and ensures that their integrated results meet the business plan.

b. <u>Monthly Review Process</u>

The process is based on demonstrated performance and manages the rolling period forward appropriate to the business through formal monthly reviews.

c. Review of Strategic Initiatives

The company monthly review includes a review of progress and resource for strategic initiatives.

d. Short- and Long-Term Alignment

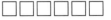

The review also ensures alignment between day-to-day events and decisions and the longer-term plans for the business and is focused on identifying business gaps and actions for their closure.

RISK MANAGEMENT

16. Risk analysis of the strategic plans and actions is systematically and rigorously conducted and includes adequate follow up to mitigate identified vulnerabilities and establish contingency plans.

a. Risk Analysis

A standard method of risk analysis, which shows the comparative criticality of risks, has been adopted and is widely used at all levels of the business on an ongoing basis.

b. Risk Management

Plans and actions exist and are updated to eliminate risk or to reduce it to manageable levels.

c. Contingency Planning

Contingency plans exist at all levels of the business to minimize the impact of known risks and to shorten disruption and recovery time.

PERFORMANCE MEASURES

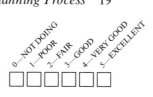

17. A process exists to assess and drive company performance to its goals and targets and to its vision through a balanced approach as perceived by its various stakeholders.

a. Integrated Measures

A balanced suite of measures is in place at the top of the company showing how well the interests of all the stakeholders are managed. This suite is the head of an integrated hierarchy of measures for the whole business that is used to monitor progress and drive action.

b. Visibility

The measures for a person or team are contained on one sheet and show trend as well as spot performance. Measures are clearly displayed for everyone to see and are designed to encourage improvement.

18. The measures are hierarchically structured and integrated so that the impact on the business of performance from any part of the organization is clearly visible and understood.

a. Team Targets

The measures at the head of the company are cascaded through all levels so that each person or team clearly understands their targets and performance expectations, including how this relates to overall company performance.

b. <u>Driving Improvement</u>

Measures are used to drive performance improvement and to encourage continuous improvement of business-relevant issues by individuals and teams.

c. <u>Relevance</u>

The measures are seen to be relevant and identify the performance and effectiveness of processes.

BEHAVIORAL CHARACTERISTICS

19. The strategic planning process is supported by a balance of cultural and behavioral development, which ensures positive team ownership of the entire plan with strong leadership and individual accountabilities.

a. <u>Leadership and Excitement</u>

The strategic planning process is led by the chief executive officer and the Leadership Team and rolled out to excite and engage all of its stakeholders.

b. <u>Ownership</u>

Performance, projects, and actions are owned at the appropriate level and are sponsored within the leadership team.

c. <u>Communication</u>

A formal communication process is used to progressively cascade the strategies throughout the business and to engage the workforce. This is actively reinforced through everyday informal communication.

2
MANAGING AND LEADING PEOPLE

PURPOSE

To develop people and their behaviors and the organizational culture and structure to deliver upper-quartile business plan performance through line management and team ownership.

Chapter Content

Integration with Strategy and All Business Processes
Leadership
People in Teams
People Development
Communication
Organization Design Development and Planning
Change Management and Learning
Consistent Working Practices
Management of Health, Safety Environment, and Community
    Relations
Performance Measures

INTEGRATION WITH STRATEGY
AND ALL BUSINESS PROCESSES

1. The values statement drives the development of the people strategy, which supports the business strategy.

a. Values Documented and Visible

The company's values are both documented and visible for all employees. They are well publicized throughout the company. This is a proactive process, which seeks to refresh the presentation regularly. The aim is to ensure ongoing use of the Values and Guiding Principles.

b. Live Them

The Leadership Team seeks to "live the values" by best role-model behavior. They seek and require similar demonstrations from their managers, supervisors, and team leaders and, thus, from all employees.

c. Culture Aligned to Values

It is recognized that the values are the glue for the organization; thus, the culture is continuously checked for alignment with the values. The employee attitude survey is an important part of this checking process.

d. Linkage to Other Strategies

The core basis of the value statements can be seen throughout the company's strategies as a thread linking them together. Key owners of the various company strategies can articulate that linkage.

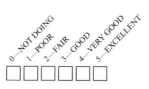

e. Trust

Trust is highly valued throughout the organization. Key behaviors are widely recognized and are likely to include open door policy; "management by walking about;" accepting of differences, including suggestions for improvement, consistency of message, and so on.

2. People strategies are well integrated with the company's overall business strategies and demonstrate the commitment to aligning all employees with the company's focus.

a. Create and Document

The people strategies for the organization are drawn up and owned by the whole of the Leadership Team. They are documented and reviewed at least annually to ensure they remain relevant.

b. Relationship to Other Strategies

People strategies are well integrated with the company's overall business strategies. They reflect the development of the organization, in particular showing the journey through transitions to greater maturity. This reflects increasing horizontal cross-functional activity linked with developing employee empowerment.

c. Leadership Team Owns

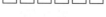

The Leadership Team, both individually and collectively, demonstrate ongoing ownership of people strategies in their day-to-day actions. Each of them can articulate the key people strategies and their role in delivering them.

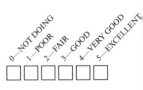

d. Awareness—Closed-Loop Feedback Test

The company seeks feedback from all employees on both the relevance and effectiveness of the people strategies and supporting actions. This is both an ongoing daily activity, as part of "good management," as well as carried out formally and regularly, e.g. at face-to-face briefing meetings, at individual performance reviews, as part of the attitude survey an so on.

e. Resource to Support

Where people strategies require resources—people and/or budget—the company can show that such resources have been made available. Where resources cannot be allocated, initiatives are prioritized on a company-wide basis.

LEADERSHIP

3. The Leadership Team articulate and demonstrate leadership, individually and collectively.

a. Understanding of Leadership versus Management

The Leadership Team know and understand leadership qualities. They are able to articulate and demonstrate the difference and balance between management and leadership. They are able to build a desire for action in the rest of the organization.

b. Situational Leadership and Maturity

The Leadership Team are able to adapt their style to fit a broad range of business as well as individual and team situations. Their leadership style is appropriate to the current situation and consistently reflects the development of the organization as it transitions to greater maturity.

c. Demonstration—Role Model

The Leadership Team, individually and collectively, are seen by the rest of the organization as role models for leadership. They demonstrate dissatisfaction with the status quo, constantly challenge and enable the organization to improve itself, and set and live up to high standards.

d. Consistent Behaviors and Accessibility

Individuals in the Leadership Team display collective behavioral responsibility. The behavior of the individuals is completely consistent with that of the team. All members of the Leadership Team are accessible to the organization.

e. Leadership Capabilities in the Future

The Leadership Team recognize that Leadership styles, skills, and abilities requirements will change over time. Processes and plans are in place to ensure that the right mix of skills and styles will be present in the team.

4. Leadership qualities are encouraged and rewarded at all levels throughout the organization.

a. <u>Identification of Leaders</u>

Employees at all levels of the organization who demonstrate leadership qualities are identified and empowered to take on challenging assignments.

b. <u>Education and Training</u>

All employees with leadership potential are given the necessary education and training to learn the required skills and behaviors.

c. <u>Encouragement, Reward, Recognition, Visibility</u>

Demonstration of leadership is encouraged in employees at all levels. Employees who meet these challenges receive appropriate recognition and rewards. Successes are celebrated and made visible to the rest of the organization.

d. <u>Leadership Opportunities and Resources</u>

The organization provides many opportunities for employees to demonstrate leadership and to put learning into practice. Resources are provided in terms of budget or people.

e. <u>Leadership Culture</u>

The culture of the organization supports the development of potential leaders, in line with these and similar behaviors. Mentors are assigned. Mutual trust and accountability are visible. Mistakes made while learning are tolerated. The rules are clear, and credit is shared.

PEOPLE IN TEAMS

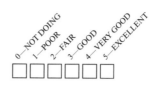

5. Teams are utilized as the primary means to direct, organize, and carry out the work.

a. Team Selection and Charter

Consistent criteria are used to select team members. Teams develop and work to an agreed Charter to satisfy the scope of their task.

b. Team Training and Team Building

Teamwork is reinforced throughout the company through the use of team-building activities. These activities are supported with training.

c. Appropriateness of Teams to Maturity Level

As the company develops from a functional organization to a more process-based structure, the organization of teams is developed to complement the changing requirements.

d. Team Performance, Results, and Recognition

The company rewards team performance, not just that of individuals. Team results are maintained and displayed by the team.

e. Teams Aligned to Business Processes

Teams are aligned to business processes, thus business needs are recognized as more important than functional or personal needs. The teams pursue continuous improvement.

6. An empowerment culture exists to support and encourage employees to meet their responsibilities.

a. <u>Process-Based Teams</u>

Teams are aligned to processes and understand their roles and responsibilities. When selected for teams, people understand the scope of their empowerment.

b. <u>Resources</u>

Management demonstrate the importance of teams through the allocation of resources to the team. Teams are educated and trained to assist skills development.

c. <u>Management Role</u>

Management understand that for empowerment to succeed, they must step back and let go. However, they continue to provide direction and guidance.

d. <u>Empowerment Increases with Maturity</u>

As the company's environment matures towards "self-managed teams," a "boundaryless" mindset develops, increasing empowerment.

e. <u>People Accept Empowerment and Are Accountable for Their Actions</u>

People openly and readily state their accountabilities and responsibilities. The environment is one of support and learning. Individuals recognize and embrace their team role.

PEOPLE DEVELOPMENT

7. The development of the people is viewed as strategically important and actively deployed.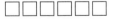

a. <u>Budget Commitment, Opportunity, and</u> <u>Resources</u>

The company has committed adequate resources, time, and finances to education and training.

b. <u>Development Planning and Measurement of</u> <u>Success</u>

Education and training are aligned with the strategic initiatives to assure the right education and training is done and that it is cost-effective. Education and training includes the principles of process and behavior change in an organization rather than just fact transfer tied to specific technology.

c. <u>Education and Training Actively Deployed</u>

The company education and training schedule is drawn up and published at least annually. The execution of the schedule is constantly tracked.

d. <u>Performance Appraisal (Individual and Team)</u>

A performance appraisal process has been established to provide employee feedback on key performance indicators that are directly linked to the company's strategies, business plan, goals, and performance of business processes. Performance appraisals are linked to the successful application of skills and knowledge gained in the education and training sessions. An appraisal process is in place that has feedback capability from all levels.

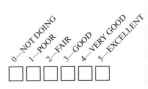

e. <u>Opportunities for Personal Growth for All on an Equal Basis</u>

The company provides the opportunity for advancement to all individuals within the organization on an equal basis with other applicants, both inside and outside the company. The company seeks applicants from a wide variety of backgrounds to ensure diversity of skills, perspectives, and opinions throughout the leadership and technical ranks.

8. The company equips its people with the core competencies and skills required for the future.

a. <u>Competencies and Skills Defined and Linked to Roles</u>

Skill types that are critical to successfully implement strategies have been identified in each business process. Competency profiles have been created for these job families. These competencies may vary but should include satisfying customer requirements, process knowledge, teamwork, innovation, mentoring, financial competency, and governance.

b. <u>Succession Planning</u>

Key positions have potential applicants within the organization that are positioned to fill openings as they occur. Career paths are clearly identified and communicated. Succession planning includes external recruitment.

c. <u>Mentoring and Coaching—Managing the Talent</u>

Mentoring and coaching of team members are well established and valued processes. Mentors meet with assigned individuals on a regular basis to review progress and give guidance on the individual's career plan.

d. <u>Developing and Retaining the Right People</u>

There is a clearly defined process for employee selection, induction, and placement. Employee development, career planning, and mentoring programs are in place and used to motivate and retain employees.

e. <u>Self-development is Encouraged and Demonstrated</u>

There is an ongoing process to assist individuals with managing their own careers within the company. Individual progress toward their career goals is reviewed at least annually as part of the company's employee-development process.

COMMUNICATION

9. Good communication is promoted up and down the management structure and across all functions and processes.

a. <u>Consistency</u>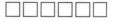

The importance of consistent, reliable, and relevant communications is recognized. Management initiate core messages and subsequently check for consistency throughout the organization.

b. Two-Way

It is recognized that communication is a two-way process. Thus, mechanisms are in place to ensure that feedback is collected and acted upon, both up and down and across the organization.

c. Natural Communication

The organization encourages "natural communication" between people. People at every level automatically give and look to receive information to help them in their jobs.

d. Communication Etiquette

The organization has educated people at all levels in how to communicate effectively. These skills are two-way, and positive communication behaviors are required from all employees.

e. Meeting Skills and Behaviors

There is a focus on the importance of meeting skills and behaviors. Training has been given. Positive meeting skills and behaviors are consistently reinforced.

10. The company has an effective communication framework.

a. Definition

There is a comprehensive communications framework laying out the frequency, content, purpose, level of detail, venues, importance of listening skills, and so on, for communication within the organization. Communication covers all levels of the organization from top to bottom, and it is regularly audited both for structure and effectiveness.

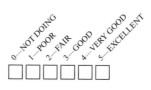

b. Measure Effectiveness and Success

The communication processes are regularly measured for effectiveness and success; this is often a part of the Attitude Survey. Results are publicized and actions taken subsequently.

c. Closed-Loop Feedback (Perception Is Reality)

The communication process actively seeks feedback from employees at all levels. There is recognition that the perception of the message by employees is their reality of what is being communicated.

d. Significance of Face-on-Face is Recognized

The key importance of face-on-face briefing is recognized and thus practiced throughout the organization at all levels.

e. Following Through with Actions/Speed of Response

A communications process actively seeks upward feedback and then ensures that answers are provided. These answers are publicized widely to maximize the benefit. Speed of answer is recognized as important. Feedback is used to tailor future communications.

ORGANIZATION DESIGN DEVELOPMENT AND PLANNING

11. **The planning and design of the organization, its role and its tasks reflect the business' maturity and future plans.**

a. <u>Alignment with Strategy</u>

The design of and planning for the organization is aligned with business strategy such that the organization is optimally structured and staffed. Organization structure, roles, and tasks reflect the maturity of the business and its characteristics.

b. <u>Simplification and Adaptability</u>

The levels in the organization structure have been minimized. The organization is flexible and adaptable to changing business conditions.

c. <u>Balancing Function against Process</u>

Organizational planning and design balances function and process. Functional depth is provided while, at the same time, recognizing the process characteristics of work. Process excellence (speed, cost, quality) is fostered by the organization design. The organization is designed to meet internal and external customer needs.

d. <u>Effective Planning</u>

The company ensures that steps are taken to gain the understanding of the case for organizational change and expectations for roles, tasks, and performance objectives.

e. <u>Compensation</u>

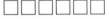

The compensation plan reflects the business philosophy and fosters the achievement of business goals and objectives in a cost-effective way. Compensation structure attracts and retains competent employees. Team-based rewards are important.

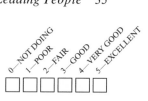

12. Employee policies and procedures are consistent with the organizational design and plans. They reflect a thought-through approach for employees and are seen to be followed.

a. Performance Management

Performance goals, time frames, and methods of measurement are documented and well understood. Employee performance is managed in an open and constructive manner.

b. Human Resource Procedures

Human resource policies and procedures are reviewed at least annually. Policies and procedures are comprehensive, fully documented, and readily accessible, and employees understand them and know where to find them. Important policies and procedures are visibly posted in the workplace.

c. Staff Planning and Resource Planning

Staffing and resource planning, including the use of temporary workforce and outsourcing, also selection and redeployment, are consistent with human resource and business strategy.

d. Employee Relations and Recognition

Excellent employee relations are an objective of the company, and management actions reinforce this. The company places an emphasis on relationships and concern for others throughout the organization. Recognition of individuals and teams is widespread.

e. <u>Employee Welfare and Quality of Life</u>

The company concerns itself with quality of life and the welfare of employees, actively improving the human side of work. Employment continuity is an articulated, communicated company objective, and effective planning reduces the negative effects of rapid change in demand and/or growth. The need for work/life balance is considered in job design.

CHANGE MANAGEMENT AND LEARNING

13. The management of change is viewed as a distinct and ongoing requirement, and is a way of life for the entire organization. All changes are planned and managed effectively.

a. <u>Education</u>

The effective implementation of change is part of the education curriculum for all employees. Leadership and management embrace change and demonstrate acceptance. Dissatisfaction with the status quo is strongly encouraged.

b. <u>Advocates and Change Agents</u>

Advocates and Change Agents ensure that individuals, teams, and groups provide a welcoming atmosphere for new ideas, and support the development and implementation of change through their behaviors and actions.

c. <u>Change Is Increasingly Accepted as a Way of Life</u>

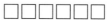

Employees are motivated and rewarded for recommending and participating in meaningful changes.

d. <u>Assessment and Readiness</u>

The need for change and expected results are validated through problem analysis and diagnosis, examination of alternative solutions, and testing/simulation of results. Education and training is always conducted prior to implementation.

e. <u>Implementation</u>

Change is planned and managed effectively, utilizing proven methodologies.

14. The company has adopted the philosophy of the learning organization. There is an active education and training program for all employees reflecting current and future business needs.

a. <u>The Need for Continual Learning</u>

The company recognizes the need, in an environment of dynamic change, for continually learning how to increase their capacity to create the future they desire and share together.

b. <u>Knowledge Management</u>

The organization recognizes the need for capturing and retaining systematic and comprehensive knowledge about the business. Knowledge is captured and built into processes and procedures.

c. Shared Learning

Learnings are captured, documented, and shared broadly. Shared learning is used to develop the capacities of individuals and teams.

d. Learning Benefits Individual Employees and the Organization

Employee development emphasizes learning that increases employee competencies and creative potential. Career planning and organization work design recognize the interdependent development of people and the business.

e. Learning Resources Available

Learning resources are readily available in a variety of formats that accommodate and cater for diverse learning styles. Learning media include a variety of delivery modes to fit work conditions/characteristics.

CONSISTENT WORKING PRACTICES

15. The policies, procedures, and practices are applied consistently and effectively throughout the company.

a. Documented and Visible

The company's working policies, procedures, and work practices are documented and visible throughout the organization.

b. Educated and Owned

All employees are educated in the significance of the working practices that apply to them, and they are properly inducted into them and receive training as necessary to deliver them.

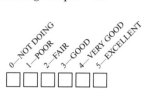

c. Relevant and Applied

The workplace policies, procedures, and practices are demonstrably relevant, and employees can be seen to be applying them day by day.

d. Traceable and Auditable

In line with best practice, all policies, procedures, and practices are easily traceable and auditable, either by internal auditors or external auditors.

e. Compliant with Widely Recognized Standards

The company aims to have policies, procedures, and practices, which are universally compliant with standards generally and widely recognized to apply to their particular industry.

16. These procedures and practices are well integrated into people's normal daily activities.

a. Actively Deployed

The policies, procedures, and practices are actively deployed in daily work by employees and their immediate Supervisors/Team Leaders.

b. Widely Understood and Demonstrated

The policies, procedures, and practices are widely understood, and employees demonstrate this during the working day as they carry out their work activities.

c. Mechanism for Review or Change

There is a straightforward and effective mechanism for reviewing and changing policies and procedures.

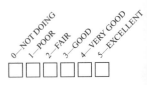

d. <u>Changes and Improvements Are Initiated by Users</u>

Users are required to maintain their local policies, procedures, and practices such that they remain up to date and relevant. The change procedure is well understood and actively utilized.

e. <u>Simplification</u>

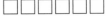

Simplification of policies, procedures, and practices is consistently encouraged from all users under the banner of "elimination of waste and increased simplification."

MANAGEMENT OF HEALTH, SAFETY, ENVIRONMENT, AND COMMUNITY RELATIONS

17. The significance of managing safety, health, and the environment is demonstrated throughout the company.

a. <u>People</u>

All employees view their own and their colleagues' safety (and indeed that of anybody on the premises) as their number one priority. The company understands the people and business benefits of a healthy workforce and supports employee well-being. Safety, Health, and Environmental awareness education and training is an ongoing requirement for all employees and is part of the induction program for new employees.

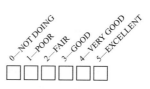

b. Compliance with Regulation and Legislation

The company knows and understands current Health, Safety, and Environmental regulations and legislative requirements. Processes are in place to ensure compliance. All employees know and understand the processes relevant to them and their work. Any changes are communicated promptly, and employees are educated and trained accordingly.

c. Tools, Auditing, and Measurement

All employees have sufficient knowledge and the proper materials and equipment to do their jobs safely and with minimum impact on the environment. Performance Measures are included in the portfolio of key business measures for the company. Regular audits are conducted in the workplace.

d. Continuous Improvement, Elimination of Waste

All employees are committed to reducing the company's impact on the environment through the promotion of best practice and the continuous elimination of waste. Opportunities for process improvements, recycling, and the reduction of waste output are constantly being identified and implemented.

e. Prevention

The company recognizes the importance of prevention in terms of Health, Safety, and Environmental problems.

18. The company demonstrates a continuous, positive commitment to the local community.

a. <u>Proactive Commitment to Community Relations</u>

There is a demonstrable proactive commitment from the management team to strengthen relations with the local community. Continuous efforts are made to earn the trust and goodwill of the community. Two-way communication with the community is in place.

b. <u>Community Validation</u>

The company is respected by the local community. The benefits brought to the community by the company are recognized. The company is seen as a good neighbor.

c. <u>Leadership</u>

Leadership ensures that everyone in the organization understands the importance and value of good community relations.

d. <u>Wide Range of Community Activities</u>

There is widespread employee involvement in communications and activities with the local community.

e. <u>Integration of Business Activity and Community Activity</u>

Where possible, business activities are supportive of community needs, and community issues are considered as part of strategic and tactical implementation plans.

PERFORMANCE MEASURES

19. There is a wide range of people performance measures that are fair and effective. These measures are balanced. They support the cultural environment for the improvement of the business. All measures have ownership and accountability and are integrated as part of a company suite.

a. <u>Best Practices</u>

A balance of people performance measures is designed to support business improvement and is integrated with Strategic Business Objectives. Support for the community is also recognized. Measures clearly identify the individual's role.

b. <u>Linkage of Education and Training Spending to Business Results</u>

People performance measures are integrated and mutually supporting across all business processes and reflect desired behaviors to ensure organizational alignment and to achieve the company's strategic objectives. Education and training spending per employee is linked to business performance measures.

c. <u>Management Ownership</u>

Performance improvement is the responsibility of the company's management team, not Human Resources. They understand that financial results are derived from operational results and develop appropriate people performance measures.

d. Range of Hard and Soft Measures

Measures of behavior, accountability, and learning are included in the individual's performance measurement matrix, along with the measurement of skills and business results. The range of business level measures usually includes attendance and employee turnover, recognizing that these reflect morale. As a minimum, the measures need to include absenteeism, retention rates, and diversity.

e. Measured Results Are Acted Upon

The management team take ownership for and analyze the gaps between desired and actual performance in all areas. The set of measures demonstrates continuous performance improvement and is benchmarked to upper-quartile performance.

20. There is a regular employee survey, the results of which are both publicized and acted upon.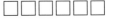

a. High Participation

Employee satisfaction and organizational climate measures are taken. High participation is a key objective.

b. Anonymity Preserved

Individual identities are not part of the employee attitude surveys and anonymity is essential. Thus the surveys are carried out in a professional manner, often utilizing external support.

c. Publicized and Communicated

The results of employee attitude surveys are published.

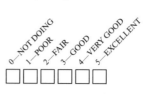

d. <u>Acted Upon</u>

Survey-related action plans for improvement should be published and implemented.

e. <u>Repeated</u>

Employee attitude and organizational climate surveys are conducted regularly and are a normal part of the company's performance improvement process. The frequency of the main survey should be at least annual.

3

DRIVING BUSINESS IMPROVEMENT

PURPOSE

Establish the comprehensive improvement architecture, which links to the company's business performance improvement program. It is used to drive business results to upper-quartile performance and beyond.

Chapter Content

Integration with Strategy
Discovery
Ownership and Involvement
Continuous Improvement
Velocity throughout Business Process
Responsiveness to Customer
Failure-Free Process
Knowledge Capture and Management
Asset Management
Innovation
Balanced Approach and Measures Hierarchy
Behavioral Characteristics

INTEGRATION WITH STRATEGY

1. The aspirations of the company and an understanding of the steps to achieve them are used to define and drive the company on a sustainable journey to Business Excellence.

a. Business Aspiration

The vision for the business has been defined using the Strategic Business Objectives as a framework. These objectives have been communicated consistently and are understood throughout the business.

b. Key Steps

The key steps required to achieve the objectives have been determined, and an associated plan has been developed. Their relative contributions and relationships are defined and understood.

c. Sequencing

Key steps have been prioritized based on the competitive priorities as determined by the strategy and business need.

d. Relationship to Value Proposition

The relationship between improvement activities and the company's Value Proposition is understood. The emphasis of the improvement activities have been focused accordingly.

e. Business Improvement Journey

A plan is in place that specifies the various improvement activities, their interrelationship, timing, and expected contribution to business improvement. The plan is owned by the Leadership Team.

2. Performance improvement activities are coordinated through Integrated Business Planning. All employees can relate improvement strategies and projects that they are involved in to the company's mission and vision statements.

a. <u>Progress Review</u>

The Leadership Team review progress against the overall improvement plan on a regular basis. The review embraces progress in terms of tasks and timing, resource requirements, budget, and benefit realization.

b. <u>Integration</u>

All improvement plans are reviewed at the relevant Integrated Business Planning element(s). All known resource requirements and expected benefits are included in the current Integrated Business Plan.

c. <u>Communication on Progress</u>

Visible performance measures and regular two-way communication meetings are used to maintain awareness on business improvement activities and progress against the Strategic Business Objectives.

d. <u>Employee Understanding</u>

Employees understand how their specific improvement projects contribute to the vision, strategic objectives, and competitive priorities of the business. This clarifies their individual role and contribution to realization of the strategy and business improvement objectives.

DISCOVERY

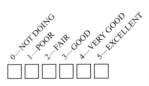

3. Competitor analysis is continuously assessed. Performance levels are understood, business goals have been established, and the business is focused on attaining upper-quartile performance or above.

a. <u>Core Business Processes</u>

The core business processes have been determined and defined. Their relative contribution and relationship to overall business performance and the competitive priorities is understood. Process owners are in place and understand their role and responsibility in terms of achievement of upper-quartile performance.

b. <u>Upper-Quartile Performance</u>

Upper-quartile performance has been researched and defined in terms of both industry sector and core business processes. This information has been used to set internal goals, objectives, and appropriate process performance metrics.

c. <u>Competitor Analysis</u>

An analysis of competitor capability and performance levels has been completed. This information has been used to identify competitive opportunities, and these have been integrated into the business improvement priorities, and the plan is continually refreshed.

d. <u>Business Goals</u>

The aspirations of the business and the Strategic Business Objectives have been developed with regard to upper-quartile and competitor performance levels.

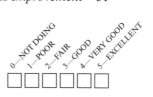

4. Benchmarking is carried out across core business processes and practices. Process owners use this knowledge to drive improvement activities.

a. <u>Benchmarking</u>

Benchmarking activities are routinely undertaken. Company and process performance are benchmarked against the best-known performers from all sectors of industry as well as internally across the business.

b. <u>Benchmarking Process</u>

The benchmarking process is documented, and clear roles and responsibilities have been defined. Information collected is shared quickly. All improvement opportunities that have been identified are quickly implemented. Visits to customers and suppliers are seen as a benchmarking opportunity and treated accordingly.

c. <u>Review Current Performance</u>

Review of the current performance compared to the benchmarked data is ongoing, and gap-closing actions and progress are reviewed as part of Integrated Business Planning.

d. <u>Sharing and Sustaining</u>

There is a formal process for implementing, sharing, and sustaining best practice within the business. The information and knowledge obtained is stored and readily accessible.

e. <u>External Critiques</u>

Critiquing in the form of external visits, assessments, and audits is used to identify and understand best practice. Associated feedback information is used to enhance existing improvement plans.

f. <u>Best Practice</u>

An understanding of future best practice is maintained via education, academic reference or papers, and relevant associations. This knowledge is used to influence the existing business improvement plan.

OWNERSHIP AND INVOLVEMENT

5. There is a formal process in place that mandates ownership and accountability of process, data, and the physical workplace to people and teams throughout the organization.

a. <u>Improvement Agenda</u>

There is widespread dissatisfaction with the status quo, and all employees can articulate the need for ongoing performance improvement.

b. <u>Formal Transfer of Ownership</u>

A structured process has been implemented that mandates employees to take ownership of their working environment. The process also provides clear expectations in terms of the standards that need to be achieved and maintained.

c. Efficient Working Environment

The importance of an efficient working environment is understood and data, information, documentation, tools, and materials are all stored with a view to ease of use and safety.

d. Team Ownership

Team-based ownership of the working environment and improvement activities have been established. Where possible and appropriate, processes have been organized to colocate the people who work in them.

6. It is widely understood that ownership and accountability are prerequisites for performance improvement.

a. Improvement Ideas

All employees contribute ideas for improvement. All ideas are reviewed, and appropriate feedback and recognition are provided in a timely fashion. The volume of ideas generated and implemented is monitored and displayed.

b. Visibility of Project Ownership

A comprehensive structure of improvement activities is in place, maintained, and communicated. This provides visibility of both ownership and the level of involvement in improvement activities.

c. Visibility of Standards

Teams have created and agreed a definition of the standards to be maintained with regard to their working environment. This definition has been communicated and is prominently displayed in their work area.

d. <u>Team Ownership</u>

Teams are used to audit the working environment against the expected standards and suggest corrective actions or improvement ideas. The teams are expected to implement all appropriate improvement actions within a reasonable timescale.

CONTINUOUS IMPROVEMENT

7. A structure and environment that ensures deployment of Continuous Improvement is in place.

a. <u>Company-Wide Involvement</u>

Continuous Improvement has become the way of life in every part of the business. All employees actively participate in improvement activities on a routine and ongoing basis.

b. <u>Strategic Alignment</u>

Improvement projects clearly state their relationship and expected contribution to the Strategy and Business Plan.

c. <u>Customer Focus</u>

The business understands both external and internal Customer requirements and ensures that these are both met and exceeded via delivery of ongoing improvement.

d. <u>Use of Teams</u>

Multifunctional, process-based teams are routinely deployed to resolve problems and generate improvement. The teams are empowered to make change within the process.

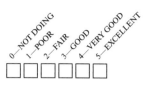

e. <u>Empowerment</u>

Employees are empowered and required to continually identify and implement improvement. They receive support and input as required from other areas of the business. This second aspect of their job is understood by everyone. Teams understand their level of authority and know at what point to seek management involvement or authorization.

f. <u>Visual Management</u>

Visual Management techniques are deployed at all levels in the organization to define standards and drive performance improvement. All relevant performance metrics and gap-closing actions are prominently displayed in the workplace.

8. An appropriate methodology exists that provides a framework for sustainable improvement.

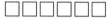

a. <u>Standard Template</u>

The company has adopted a standard template to capture and communicate improvement projects. This template is displayed prominently in the area related to the process.

b. <u>Benefits</u>

Improvement projects detail expected benefits. These benefits may relate to quality, cost, delivery, safety, environment, and so on. A register of expected and realized benefits for all past and current projects is in place and maintained.

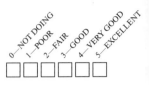

c. <u>Customer/Supplier Agreements</u>

Formal customer/supplier agreements, such as Service Level Agreements, exist and are maintained for both external and internal relationships. The agreements detail requirements and define key elements of the relationship.

d. <u>Supplier/Customer Relationships</u>

Ongoing measures are in place to monitor input, process, and output activity. These measures are routinely reviewed and improvement actions and goals are established. Changes and improvements are formalized using modifications to Customer/Supplier agreements.

e. <u>Measures of Completion</u>

All improvement projects or activities have a stated "measure of completion." Process measurement continues until the measure of completion has been achieved. For many projects, this means that the financial objectives have been realized.

f. <u>Ongoing Measurement</u>

Ongoing measurement remains in place to ensure that the improved condition is sustained. New performance standards are integrated into associated business and planning rules and working procedures.

VELOCITY THROUGHOUT BUSINESS PROCESSES

9. The business embraces Lean as its means of understanding customer value and attaining upper-quartile velocity.

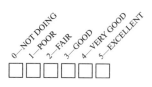

a. <u>Lean Principles</u>

There is a common understanding of Lean principles and a relentless pursuit of waste elimination throughout the business.

b. <u>Velocity</u>

Upper-quartile velocity has been determined for all core processes. Improvement objectives have been set accordingly, and appropriate gap-closing action plans are in place.

c. <u>Application of Lean Mind-Set</u>

Significant Customer or business improvements have been delivered using lean thinking. These improvements have increased velocity, and waste has been removed. The benefits achieved can be related to the business strategy.

d. <u>Value</u>

Value is understood and has been defined from the Customer perspective. Value-add and non-value-add steps are identified as part of any improvement. The focus, therefore, is on the reduction of non-value-add steps.

e. <u>Lean Deployment</u>

The five steps to Lean are understood and are being used to drive progressive change to achieve Lean processes. This has ensured a logical, structured, and systematic approach to process improvement.

f. <u>Understanding Waste</u>

Everyone understands the "seven types of waste." Employees can articulate relevant examples of each type of waste in their working environment and can explain how waste has been reduced through improvement actions.

g. Value Stream Mapping

Value Stream Mapping is used to determine velocity, and all areas of the business can demonstrate improvement activities that have focused on increasing velocity through elimination of waste. The velocity of all core processes is measured and tracked to ensure improvement.

h. Plan, Do, Check, Act

Plan, Do, Check, Act, or more advanced methodology, is used to provide improvement project structure. The methodology is understood and applied by all employees in all areas of the business; Plan, Do, Check, Act is supported by accurate process data that are collected locally by process team members.

10. The concept of pull has been understood and appropriately applied throughout the business.

a. Appraisal of Pull

Pull from customer demand is seen as a competitive advantage and as a means of contributing to the Value Proposition. A benefit analysis of pull has been completed to find the most appropriate economical balance.

b. Pull from Customer Demand

Where applicable, the business has a plan to move to pull from customer demand. There is an understanding of how this can be most effectively achieved and of the resultant benefits.

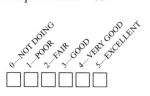

c. <u>Kanban</u>

Techniques such as Kanban are used to drive re-plenishment in processes where appropriate. Where Kanban is used, people can articulate calculation methods and understand that the Kanban quantity is itself waste and hence a further opportunity for improvement. Where Kanban is used, its rules are defined and all violations measured.

d. <u>Planning</u>

Planners understand and can articulate the planning approach and procedures for pull from customer demand. Where required, a plan is in place to accommodate the change to pull from customer demand.

e. <u>Education</u>

A Lean education program that included all employees, key suppliers, and partner customers has been completed. The program scope includes ongoing education for new employees.

RESPONSIVENESS TO CUSTOMER

11. The business has gained competitive advantage from rapid and cost-effective response to customer requirements from flexible and agile processes.

a. <u>Agility</u>

The concepts of Agility are understood and can be articulated throughout the organization. Where appropriate, these concepts have been applied to increase flexibility and improve responsiveness.

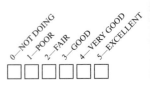

b. Design for Agility Understood

The concept of designing agile processes is understood and has been applied where appropriate. Evidence of successful application is available.

c. Agile Improvement Projects

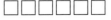

Improvement projects completed or in progress have increased flexibility and the business's ability to effectively respond to change.

d. Constraint Management

Where appropriate, traditional Constraint Management has been replaced by techniques associated with providing enhanced flexibility. These techniques are being used to drive ongoing improvement in terms of flexibility and responsiveness.

e. Extended Supply Chain

Agile thinking is being applied throughout the supply chain. Customers and suppliers are involved in associated improvement activities.

12. The business can demonstrate its ability to reconfigure processes and organization either to respond to or stimulate change in the market place for competitive advantage.

a. Scenario Plans

Scenario plans have been developed that, when required, can be implemented to achieve rapid deployment of process change. Consequences have been evaluated using Integrated Business Planning.

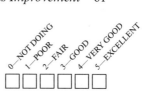

b. <u>Flexibility of Labor</u>

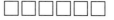

Flexibility of labor is viewed as a competitive advantage. A structured plan is in place to increase flexibility in terms of both skills and working arrangements.

c. <u>Value Manipulation</u>

The steps in processes where value is added have been identified. The associated activities can be manipulated to increase product/service variety, maintain flexibility, and minimize the increase in non-value-add activity and cost.

d. <u>Design for Product Agility</u>

Design for Agility concepts are applied to new products, service, and equipment. All involved in the new product or service introduction process can articulate these concepts. Examples of application of the concepts in each area are available.

FAILURE-FREE PROCESSES

13. There is a formal process in place to reduce variation that can be applied to all types of processes throughout the business.

a. <u>Process-Based Measurement</u>

Process-based measurement is in place. These measures are used to provide feedback on the ongoing performance of the process and to drive improvement through the reduction in process variation.

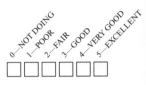

b. <u>Process Variation</u>

Process variation is measured and is continually being reduced. Statistical problem-solving techniques are deployed to reduce variation of process activities toward Six-Sigma performance levels.

c. <u>Statistical Process Control</u>

Process control and consistency is seen as fundamental to quality and performance improvement. Statistical process control is understood and used throughout the business to maintain control and prevent process failure.

d. <u>Root Cause Analysis</u>

Root Cause Analysis and associated tools and techniques are used extensively throughout the business. The causes of failure and deviation are routinely identified, and Root Cause Analysis is used to determine and implement a permanent corrective action.

e. <u>Quality</u>

Clear quality standards have been agreed and defined. Defect prevention rather than detection is the norm. Quality is designed and built into the product and process. The Cost of Quality is understood and can be shown.

14. Techniques are deployed to measure and control inputs and process capability to ensure the output requirements are met.

a. <u>Input Measures</u>

The importance of controlling key process inputs is understood. The critical attributes of these inputs have been determined. Appropriate controlling measures are in place, and these input-based measures are used to drive ongoing process improvement.

b. <u>Standard Operating Procedures</u>

Standard Operating Procedures exist for all processes and are used to provide process consistency. A procedure for controlling process change is in place, and this procedure is known and understood by all employees.

c. <u>Closed-Loop Controls</u>

Closed-Loop Controls are applied to all improvement actions. These controls are used to ensure process improvement or elimination of process failure. They are sustained, and relevant process control parameters have been redefined.

d. <u>Input/Output Requirements</u>

A structured approach has been used to identify and define process input and output requirements. These requirements have been built into the appropriate Customer/Supplier agreements.

e. <u>Continuous Improvement</u>

Continuous Improvement tools and techniques are in place and are used routinely by employees to resolve process problems and improve process performance.

KNOWLEDGE CAPTURE AND MANAGEMENT

15. All knowledge and learning is formally captured and integrated into business processes and the evolving knowledge database.

a. Knowledge Capture

A process exists to capture and disseminate knowledge. This process is owned and reviewed to ensure effectiveness. Knowledge is captured from both success and failure. All knowledge obtained is stored in the appropriate area of the business's knowledge database.

b. Best Practice

Learning from problem solving and Continuous Improvement activities is captured and used to share and develop best practice throughout the organization. Examples and successes are documented and publicized throughout the business.

c. Education

Employees are encouraged to attend relevant educational courses and external events. The importance of sharing and applying the learning from such activities is understood.

d. External Knowledge

The business realizes the importance of seeking every possible opportunity to gain knowledge from Customers, suppliers, consumers, and competitors. Both formal and informal approaches are applied. All knowledge gained is shared with appropriate parties and made available throughout the business.

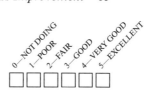

e. <u>Benchmarking</u>

Benchmarking activities are seen as an excellent source of knowledge. The benchmarking process makes the necessary provision for capturing and sharing the knowledge obtained from all associated activities.

16. All employees understand the importance and responsibility of transferring their individual knowledge into the process or business.

a. <u>Process Change</u>

Employees evaluate the process carried out versus the standard operating procedures on a routine basis. Reasons for changes to the process are captured and used to drive improvement to Standard Operating Procedures via a formal change control.

b. <u>Knowledge Sharing</u>

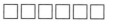

Knowledge is not seen as a way of assuming power or control, and hence all employees actively share and transfer their individual knowledge with each other and into both the process and the systems.

c. <u>Data</u>

Data collection and collation is seen as an important source of information and knowledge. Relevant data are captured on a routine basis to increase knowledge of both the capability and the performance of the process.

d. Training

Internal training programs incorporate latest knowledge and skills. This ensures that the latest best practice is shared formally and in an appropriate manner. The process for development and maintenance of training programs includes a requirement to obtain the latest knowledge.

ASSET MANAGEMENT

17. There is a formal management process in place to control and protect all business equipment.

a. Equipment Ownership

Ownership of equipment has been clearly defined. The designated owners are held accountable for the condition, performance, and improvement of their equipment.

b. Maintenance Planning

Equipment owners are involved in maintenance planning. Equipment is released in accordance with the agreed schedule, and regular checks are used to maintain safety, performance, and condition.

c. Asset Control

All equipment is subject to regular audits to confirm existence and operational status. Audit results are reflected in the appropriate financial records. Actions and recommendations arising from the audits are passed to the equipment owner for implementation.

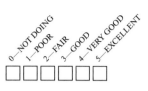

d. Planned Maintenance

A planned maintenance program with an 18- to 24-month horizon is in place for all productive equipment and plant based on demonstrated, preventative, and predicted data. Adherence to the planned maintenance schedule is measured and routinely reviewed. Planned maintenance activity is related to equipment reliability on an ongoing basis. The relationship is used to determine future maintenance plans.

18. The formal process engenders ownership of assets by the people who use them across the whole business.

a. Predictive Tools

Critical equipment has been defined, and appropriate predictive tools are in use to minimize risk of failure and determine stocking requirements in terms of spare parts.

b. Business Systems

Performance of the business systems is monitored, and findings are routinely reviewed. Problem areas have been identified, and improvement plans are in place. A process exists whereby user feedback is actively sought and acted upon.

c. Total Productive Maintenance

Key equipment is subject to Total Productive Maintenance. All relevant employees are involved in Total Productive Maintenance activity, and training programs exist to develop the associated skills and competencies. Teams perform routine maintenance checks, tasks, and inspections. Overall Equipment Effectiveness is measured and improved.

d. Reliability-Centered Maintenance

"Mean Time Between Failure" and "Mean Time to Recover" are key business performance measures. Technical maintenance activities are prioritized using these measures. An associated improvement plan is in place, and continuous improvement in both areas can be demonstrated. The maintenance team, in accordance with the stated equipment reliability, manages inventory of critical spares.

INNOVATION

19. There is a formal process for the identification and deployment of business transformation programs to drive step-change improvement.

a. Strategic Alignment

Leaders ensure that the business is actively seeking transformational opportunities that support the strategic agenda of the business. The Leadership Team recognizes the importance of innovation and encourages innovative thinking.

b. Innovation Search

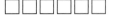

A proactive process has been established that ensures appropriate emphasis and time is allocated to identification and evaluation of relevant transformational opportunities. Various approaches for seeking out potential opportunities are in place. Innovation involves risk, so a procedure exists to protect those that may fail.

c. <u>Evaluation Process</u>

There is a formal process for evaluating, selecting, and prioritizing potential opportunities. All relevant ideas are evaluated, and their impact and relationship to strategy are understood.

d. <u>Implementation Structure</u>

The value and importance of an effective implementation process are understood. An appropriate implementation methodology is in place and facilitates successful implementation of change.

e. <u>Progress Review</u>

Implementation plans for transformational change programs are integrated with and reviewed via Integrated Business Planning.

20. The owners of core processes understand and fulfill their leadership role in terms of focusing and facilitating innovation.

a. <u>Process Innovation</u>

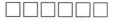

The business has developed an approach to process innovation that is complementary to continuous improvement activities. Process innovations have generated step-change improvement. Innovation in the process is driven by improvement reviews.

b. <u>Ambition</u>

Benchmarking and external research are both seen as ways of generating ambition and creating a passion for improvement outside of the internally driven improvement program.

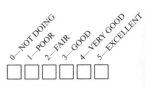

c. <u>Third parties</u>

Third parties are used to critique improvement programs and provide an external contribution to process innovation.

d. <u>Paradigms</u>

Paradigms that are holding the business back have been identified, understood, and challenged in a structured manner. All areas of the business are encouraged to contribute to step-change improvement through innovative thinking.

BALANCED APPROACH AND MEASURES HIERARCHY

21. There is a clear hierarchical link between the suite of measures for each process team and the company scorecard.

a. <u>Alignment</u>

All measures are integrated, consistent, and drive toward delivery of the vision and strategy. Measures are periodically reviewed for relevance, accuracy, tolerances, and targets as performance improves and new benchmark data are obtained.

b. <u>Balance</u>

Differing and competing key performance measures have been integrated into one combined company scorecard. This has required reconciliation of any potential conflict between measures while ensuring that the appropriate emphasis and importance has been given to each of the measures.

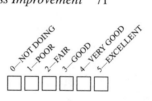

c. <u>Hierarchy</u>

A performance measurement hierarchical structure has been created and is used to show the linkage of measures from the top to the bottom of the business. The hierarchy has been communicated and is widely understood throughout the business.

d. <u>Linkage</u>

Employees understand and can articulate the linkage and fit of local process and result-based measures to overall business performance and achievement of vision. The linkage is shown visually on team boards.

e. <u>Use of Measures</u>

Measures are used for learning, to identify problems, and to focus and drive continuous improvement. Periodically, and as performance improves or new benchmarked data are obtained, measures are reviewed for relevance, accuracy, tolerances, and targets.

22. **This suite of performance measures includes both results and process measures and is used for driving performance improvement while providing management control.**

a. <u>Velocity Ratio</u>

Velocity Ratio is used as a key measure for all core business processes. The company has a stated objective to increase core process velocity.

b. <u>Agility</u>

Process responsiveness is measured and improved for those processes or activities where process agility is required as a competitive priority.

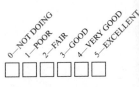

c. Cost

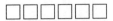

The impact of improvements is reflected and monitored in terms of cost benefits. Optimizing value-add activities are providing simultaneous benefits from growth, productivity, cash, and margin.

d. Process Improvement Activity

The number of improvement ideas being both generated and implemented is being continuously measured and is consistent with objectives.

e. Added Value

The value added per employee is being measured on an ongoing basis and showing an improving trend.

BEHAVIORAL CHARACTERISTICS

23. There is a commitment to excellence and passion for Continuous Business Improvement.

a. Management of Continuous Improvement

Management are fully supportive of Continuous Improvement activities.

b. Fact-Based Decisions

Decisions are made and justified using the relevant performance measures. All performance measures have clearly defined owners who have signed off on the method of calculation and the source(s) of data as being timely and correct.

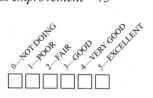

c. <u>Ambition</u>

Management continuously articulates an ambition to be the best within their chosen proposition. Milestones are used to stage the journey, and everyone understands the need for excellence.

d. <u>Goals</u>

Management is continuously seeking new opportunities to raise performance and sets goals accordingly. Continuous Improvement and step-change improvement activities are routinely deployed throughout the business to set new performance standards.

24. The organization values experimentation, breakthrough, thinking, and open-mindedness.

a. <u>Learning Environment</u>

Management actively seeks every opportunity to learn new tools and techniques. New ideas are quickly reviewed and trialed, and learning from others is seen as a strength.

b. <u>Best-Practice Visits</u>

Management actively encourages best-practice visits and research. These visits are not just at the business level but also at the process level. Best-practice visits are used to adjust targets and set new goals.

c. <u>Process Knowledge</u>

Extended process knowledge is seen as essential. The process teams that include suppliers and customers work closely together to transfer knowledge and hence understand where opportunities may exist for improvement.

d. <u>Research and Experimentation</u>

Resource investment for both external and internal research and experimentation activities is made available on an ongoing basis. Investment in research is aligned to competitive priorities and strategy.

4

INTEGRATED BUSINESS PLANNING

PURPOSE

To establish an holistic business management process that realigns company plans in response to change, to optimize financial performance. It drives gap-closing actions to address competitive priorities, upper-quartile performance, and to deliver management commitments and strategy. As such it is the mechanism that provides visibility and control for Corporate Performance Management.

Chapter Content

Integrated Business Planning Structure
Summary and Integration of the Business Reviews
Integrated Reconciliation
Management Business Review
Strategy Alignment and Deployment
Management of Risk and Contingency Planning
Financial Integration
Performance Measurement
Behavioral Characteristics
BUSINESS PERFORMANCE MEASURES

INTEGRATED BUSINESS PLANNING STRUCTURE

1. There is an Integrated Business Planning process that ensures the business is perpetually managed to meet strategies, goals, and commitments in response to changing conditions.

a. The Management Process

This is the management and decision-making process for the business and, as such, the process owner is the CEO or most senior management executive—the business head for the business entity.

b. Frequency and Horizon

Plans are reviewed monthly covering a rolling business horizon established to appropriately manage the business, with a minimum of 18, but typically 24 months. The focus is on managing the medium to longer term.

c. Business Agenda

Review agendas, for each element in the process, are focused on delivering the Value Proposition and competitive priorities as well as addressing operational issues and business commitments.

d. Policy

A concise written policy is used to provide a clear statement of management commitment to this style of business management. It defines purpose, frequency, horizon, process elements, ownership, participants, and expected outcomes.

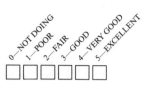

2. **The process comprises a series of integrated and interdependent business reviews, which are structured and focused recognizing the nature of the business and its organizational accountabilities.**

a. Process Definition

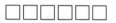

The process has been mapped, clearly showing the elements of the process, data flow, responsibilities, timing, and decision points.

b. Business Accountabilities

The process is structured in support of business accountabilities. Those accountable for delivering business plans preside over their respective element of the process. Each element and associated business review has an identified process owner who is responsible for process development and excellence.

c. Participants Clearly Identified

The participants for each element of the process have been identified. This includes the chairperson, facilitator, and cross-functional members engaged in the preparatory cycle and the business review.

d. Monthly Process with Predefined Activity Dates

This is a monthly process with a calendar maintaining 6 to 12 months' visibility. This enables all participants to manage their time, recognizing their involvement in the process, and avoiding schedule conflict.

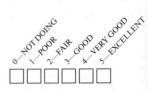

e. Global, Regional and Multientity Businesses

In global, regional, or multientity businesses, the process design has been appropriately applied to enable an effective monthly process in this more complex environment. It recognizes disparate organizational accountabilities and geography.

f. Style and Media

Particularly with dispersed geography, style and media in conducting these business reviews must be practical without sacrificing effectiveness.

3. Each business review encompasses an assessment of demonstrated performance, future plans with clearly defined supportive data, and issues or opportunities arising.

a. Data Requirements are Defined

Inputs, agenda, and outputs for each element of the process are clearly identified, as are the linkages between the elements and the required communication.

b. Families and Analysis

The reviews are conducted at a level of analysis appropriate to a business review. Often this means product or technology families or natural business segments.

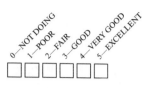

c. <u>Emphasis on Assumptions</u>

Each element of the process requires a comprehensive and documented set of facts and assumptions of which the numbers are a result. This enables understanding of the thinking and sensitivities underpinning future plans. Comparison with actual occurrences enhances understanding of results and enables ongoing validation of assumptions.

d. <u>Focus on Change</u>

Being a continuous planning process of monthly iterations, each review focuses on understanding what has changed since the prior cycle and the issues and opportunities arising. Changes to the plans should be explained and accompanied by changes to the appropriate assumptions.

e. <u>Management Information</u>

The data is filtered and summarized to focus the issues; visibility of trends and comparatives are enhanced through graphics; change, key assumptions, risks, opportunities, gaps, and recommendations are all articulated to enable review and decision making.

SUMMARY AND INTEGRATION OF THE BUSINESS REVIEWS

4. The Product Management Review manages performance, progress, and change, and ensures ownership for Product Management plans. Commitment is made to an updated plan with respect to deliverables, timing, and cost.

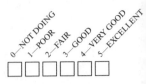

a. <u>Definition of Scope</u>

The Product Management Review is where product portfolio projects and associated activities to deliver the product/category/brand strategies are reviewed and managed. This review provides management control over the process described in Chapter 5.

b. <u>Roles</u>

The executive accountable for product strategy chairs the review. A Product Coordinator has been appointed to facilitate this element of the process—to coordinate the preparation cycle, facilitate the review, and actively participate in Integrated Reconciliation.

c. <u>Preparation</u>

Learning from demonstrated performance, update of project status, management of resources, planning assumptions, project filtering, and identification of commitment gaps are all established to enable an effective Product Management Review.

d. <u>Performance</u>

Performance is measured to establish the reliability of the process to deliver projects on time to both supply chain and market. Perfect project delivery performance meets the standard as defined in Chapter 5.

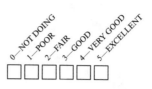

e. Review

The accountable executive (chairperson) uses the review to validate plans; manage change, risk, and opportunity; and ensure that business commitments will be met or that gap-closing actions are established. Decisions are taken and the Product Management plans are agreed.

f. Communication

The Product Management plan together with appropriate commentary is communicated as an output from the Product Management Review to subsequent elements of the process. Integration issues that impact elsewhere in the process will be identified and addressed through Integrated Reconciliation.

5. The Demand Review manages performance and ensures ownership for market and customer plans. Commitment is made to an updated demand plan in respect to volumes, revenue, and margins.

a. Definition of Scope

The Demand Review is where the multiple views of demand originating from Marketing, Sales, Supply Chain, and history are reconciled. This review provides management control over the process described in Chapter 6.

b. Roles

The executive accountable for sales revenue and margin plans chairs the review. A Demand Manager/Planner has been appointed to facilitate this element of the process—to coordinate the preparation cycle, facilitate the review, and actively participate in Integrated Reconciliation.

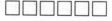

c. <u>Preparation</u>

Learning from demonstrated performance, up-date of demand plans and assumptions, modeling of opportunities, and identification of commitment gaps are all established to enable an effective Demand Review.

d. <u>Performance</u>

Execution of the demand plan is measured to establish sales performance and demand planning capability. Sales plan performance meets the standard as defined in Chapter 6.

e. <u>Review</u>

The accountable executive (chairperson) uses the review to validate plans; manage change, risk, and opportunity; and ensure that business commitments will be met or that gap-closing actions are established. Decisions are taken and the demand plan agreed.

f. <u>Communication</u>

The demand plan together with appropriate commentary is communicated as an output from the Demand Review, to subsequent elements of the process. Integration issues that impact elsewhere in the process will be identified and addressed through Integrated Reconciliation.

6. The Supply Review manages performance, capability and flexibility, and alternative supply scenarios. Commitment is made to an achievable Supply Plan in response to Product Management Plans and Demand Management requirements (including customer satisfaction) while managing resources and costs.

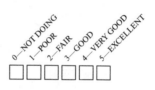

a. <u>Definition of Scope</u>

The Supply Review addresses all aspects of the supply chain and its capability to respond to demand. This review provides management control over the processes described in Chapters 7, 8, and 9.

b. <u>Roles</u>

The executive accountable for supply chain plans chairs the review. A Supply Planning Manager has been appointed to facilitate this element of the process—to coordinate the preparation cycle, facilitate the review, and actively participate in Integrated Reconciliation.

c. <u>Preparation</u>

Demonstrated performance and improvement plans, supply chain capability, inventory and/or lead time strategies and planning assumptions have been established; alternative supply plans modeled, balanced to resources; and commitment gaps identified to enable an effective review.

d. <u>Performance</u>

Aggregate supply plan performance is measured to establish reliability of the supply chain and supply planning capability. Aggregate supply plan performance meets the standard, as defined in Chapters 7 and 8.

e. <u>Review</u>

The accountable executive (chairperson) uses the review to appraise alternative plans in response to demand and product management requirements and changes in distribution channel inventory. Change, risk, and opportunity is managed to ensure that business commitments will be met or that gap-closing actions are established. Decisions are taken and the supply plan agreed.

f. <u>Communication</u>

The supply plan together with appropriate commentary is communicated as an output from the review to subsequent elements of the process. Integration issues, which impact elsewhere in the process, will be identified and addressed through Integrated Reconciliation.

INTEGRATED RECONCILIATION

7. Integrated Reconciliation takes place continuously to address business-wide issues requiring resolution. Integration issues are managed from a total business perspective to reoptimize the business in response to change.

a. <u>Definition of Scope</u>

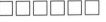

Integrated Reconciliation addresses issues that could not be resolved in the Product Management, Demand, or Supply Reviews and require broader business-wide engagement.

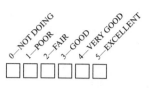

b. <u>Roles</u>

The Integrated Business Planning Process Leader, involving others depending on the issues and scenarios under consideration, facilitates Integrated Reconciliation.

c. <u>Manage Trade-Offs</u>

Where one process element is unable (within established constraints) to satisfy the requirement of another, a business-wide perspective is applied to derive the best overall solution.

d. <u>Modeling Facilitates Resolution and Optimization</u>

Integrated Reconciliation is undertaken through one-to-one and small group activity. Computer-based modeling capability is used to evaluate alternative scenarios.

e. <u>Drives Gap Closing</u>

This continuous reconciliation activity recognizes business-wide gaps versus business plan and strategy and develops gap-closing solutions and/or recommendations.

8. Approved company-wide projects are monitored and evaluated for their impact on the business.

a. <u>Definition of Scope</u>

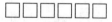

All major company projects and initiatives are monitored through this process. Those that cannot be assigned to a specific review are consolidated and communicated through the Integrated Reconciliation.

b. <u>Roles</u>

The Integrated Business Planning Process Leader updates and publishes the status of company-wide projects together with implications.

c. <u>Strategic and Integration Fit</u>

The purpose and strategic fit of each project/initiative, their alignment to other improvement projects, and their impact on operational plans can be articulated.

d. <u>Visibility for Resource Management</u>

These projects are visible to each process element to enable their impact on activities and resources to be appraised.

e. <u>Assess Viability</u>

Information is provided to the Management Business Review on status and viability of these projects in addition to all other outputs from the process. This enables visibility, prioritization, and realism in business initiative planning.

9. Financial projections derived from all preceding plans are an integral element of the process. Stand-alone financial forecasting has been eliminated.

a. <u>Definition of Scope</u>

Financial projections out to the process horizon are derived for revenue, profit, cash flow, and other selected financial data as required monthly for effective business decision making.

b. <u>Roles</u>

The Chief Financial Officer/Finance Director is a key stakeholder and owner of this element of the process, recognizing that Integrated Business Planning is the basis of all financial projections within the Integrated Business Planning horizon.

c. <u>One Set of Numbers</u>

Financial forecasts are based on the same source data. Demand, supply, and product management take responsibility for evaluating their plans—price, costs, expenses, head count, and so on, and the impact tested and validated at each respective process review. This enables increased understanding of the financial implications, allowing transparency and accountability.

d. <u>Financial Buildup</u>

Revenue, cost of sales, and gross margin is built up using aggregate family- or subfamily-level detail. Financial data are included within the Integrated Business Planning database for ease of calculation.

e. <u>Financial Appraisal</u>

Financial evaluation is consolidated and judgment applied with respect to overheads and other financial considerations not addressed at prior reviews. Financial assumptions are explicit and expressed. Dependence on historical financial appraisal and detailed variance analysis as the basis of management decision making has been largely removed. However, historical data are used to test and improve the integrity of financial assumptions.

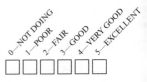

f. <u>Financial Opportunity and Risk</u>

Financial opportunity and risk are assessed and reviewed together with appropriate contingencies. The financial implications of change arising through the monthly cycle are understood and articulated.

10. A Reconciliation Review is conducted to assess the outcome of this process cycle, the status of reconciliation issues, and to identify the focus for the Management Business Review.

a. <u>Definition of Scope</u>

The latest view of the operational and financial position of the business and the achievement of business goals and commitments is reviewed throughout the process horizon.

b. <u>Roles</u>

This review is conducted between the Integrated Business Planning Process Leader, the Financial Controller, and other representatives from the total process, depending on the issues arising.

c. <u>Understanding of Change</u>

Change since the prior month's Management Business Review is highlighted, together with the impact of that change on the business.

d. <u>Focus on Issues</u>

The issues arising through this cycle are summarized together with their status. Gaps versus commitments are clarified, together with the status of gap-closing actions.

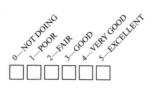

e. Preparation for the Management Business Review

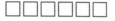

The Management Business Review agenda should be focused on those issues arising from this cycle that require communication or decision making.

MANAGEMENT BUSINESS REVIEW

11. The Management Business Review is owned and chaired by the CEO or business head and comprises the Leadership Team. The review assesses performance, trends, commitment gaps, and gap-closing proposals as an integral element of Corporate Performance Management. Decisions are taken, direction is provided and communicated for action.

a. Definition of Scope

The latest view of the operational and financial position of the business through the process horizon is reviewed together with the achievement of business strategies, goals, and commitments. The focus is on change since last month, the impact of change, the progress of actions, and the issues prepared at the Reconciliation Review.

b. Roles

The CEO or most senior management executive chairs the review, which is facilitated by the Integrated Business Planning Process Leader.

c. <u>Address the Issues</u>

Issues are addressed as presented and the required decisions taken. Gaps are reviewed versus commitments together with the status of gap-closing actions. The review provides direction on further gap closing and improvement activity, and the updated integrated plans are approved.

d. <u>Long-Term Focus</u>

The business must manage the longer-term commitments and business goals while delivering short-term results. Balance of time must be weighted to longer term issues in recognition that issues managed outside the "reactionary zone" will minimize short-term issues and increase confidence in the achievement of financial commitments.

e. <u>Communication</u>

The approved plans are communicated as an output from the review together with clear understanding of decisions taken and appropriate commentary. Ongoing integration issues and gap-closing actions will continue to be addressed through Integrated Reconciliation.

STRATEGY ALIGNMENT AND DEPLOYMENT

12. Throughout the process, strategy deployment is monitored, and leadership for the strategy is demonstrated.

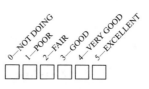

a. <u>Strategic Framework</u>

The strategic framework of value proposition, competitive priorities, and strategic direction has influenced process design and business focus.

b. <u>Visible Strategy</u>

As a part of the scorecard review, at each element of the process, key performance drivers indicate whether strategic initiatives are on track and are being achieved.

c. <u>Monitoring</u>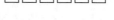

Status of strategic programs and assumptions are monitored to enable continuous review. Changes are identified early, and the impact on the business, including resources and financial performance, is evaluated.

d. <u>Focus by Exception</u>

While the monthly process is not a full strategic review, it will highlight, by exception, those strategies or programs that require management.

13. At each process review, plans are checked
    for congruence with strategy.

a. <u>Strategy Is Understood</u>

Strategy pertinent to each process review is explicit. All participants understand and can articulate the strategy, the key underlying assumptions, and the impact on the business.

b. <u>Strategy as the Driver</u>

Strategy provides the direction and framework against which proposed plans and actions are tested.

c. <u>Gap-Closing Activity</u>

Gaps between the latest bottom-up view and strategic commitments are a specific focus for each process review, resulting in gap-closing activity.

d. <u>Strategy Deviations</u>

Changes to key business facts and assumptions that could impact strategic direction will be identified and addressed through the process.

MANAGEMENT OF RISK AND CONTINGENCY PLANNING

14. Management of Risk and Contingency planning is evident throughout the process.

a. <u>Facts and Assumptions</u>

Assumptions developed for each element of the process must be routinely tested and validated. This enables appraisal of proposed plans for realism; either the plans are changed or potential risks and opportunities are declared.

b. <u>Risks and Opportunities</u>

Having identified risks and opportunities, plans are developed to negate the risks or exploit the opportunities.

c. <u>Alternative Solutions</u>

Wherever there is a level of uncertainty about the future, "what-if" scenarios are analyzed and supported by actionable contingency plans. Resulting upside and downside plans are communicated through the process.

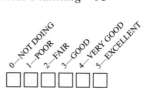

d. Managing the Risks

Upside and downside plans are reviewed for impact throughout the process. Significant issues
arising will be managed through Integrated
Reconciliation to find the best business-wide
solution, recognizing the trade-offs, while understanding and accepting the cost of uncertainty.

e. Process Capability

Achievement of past plans is evaluated against
agreed tolerances thereby establishing process
capability and the underlying level of risk. By
addressing process bias and variability, risks and
associated tolerances are reduced.

FINANCIAL INTEGRATION

**15. The annual plan is derived directly from
the Integrated Business Planning process
and extracted close to the start of
the financial year.**

a. Source of Data

The Annual Plan is derived from the Integrated
Business Planning plans. It is recognized that
Annual Plans are a "snapshot" in time, but the
business must continuously reoptimize in response to change.

b. <u>Integrated Process</u>

There is no stand-alone exercise for the generation of sales and supply plans as part of an annual planning process. The Annual Plan will require detail in addition to that generated to support the monthly process, such as expense budgets, and this is treated as an extension of Integrated Business Planning.

c. <u>Rolling Business Horizon</u>

The rolling horizon allows understanding of the next budget year to grow over many months.

d. <u>Process Effectiveness</u>

Strategy is established and business ambition understood. Demonstrated performance, plans, assumptions, and sensitivities are reviewed monthly. The issues are understood and are reducing or eliminating the need and time required for added analysis and debate. The time to prepare the Annual Plan is significantly reduced.

e. <u>Timing</u>

The Annual Plan can be extracted from the rolling process much closer to corporate review dates, and hence the start of the financial year, due to the familiarity and confidence in the process and data. This ensures maximum validity of the assumptions that will be used.

16. The business cost structures support effective business decision making through the process.

a. <u>Product Costs</u>

The source of product costs is the accurate operational database.

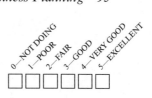

b. Integrated Transactional Data

Operational transactions drive entries in the financial ledgers to ensure closed-loop control and integration of operational and financial data. Design of the enterprise system and use of technology allows transaction processing to be as close to real time as possible such that the enterprise costing and financial systems reflect reality.

c. Understanding of Cost Drivers

Activity Based Management is practiced to ensure clear understanding of true cost drivers in the business and correct assessment of business scenarios modeled through the process.

d. Financial Analysis

Financial analysis and data is readily available to support costed what-if scenarios enabling evaluation in the process.

e. Timeliness of Financial Reporting

Month-end close is efficient to enable timely generation of financial data in support of the monthly process.

PERFORMANCE MEASUREMENT

17. **A balanced set of measures exists to manage and improve the Integrated Business Planning process and performance of the business. All measures have ownership and accountability and are integrated as part of a company suite to drive business improvement.**

a. <u>Scorecard Review</u>

Review of critical elements from the company scorecard is a key focus of the Management Business Review.

b. <u>Integrated Structure</u>

A structure of measures has been defined for each element of the process. Care has been taken to ensure they support the strategy, are complementary from a business integration perspective, and that conflicting functional measures are managed.

c. <u>Ownership and Accountability</u>

Performance measures are an early focus in each review to ensure understanding and learning from past performance as a driver for improvement. Ownership and accountability are clearly defined.

d. <u>Improvement Activities</u>

Performance improvement activities are coordinated through the Integrated Business Planning process to ensure a consistent and aligned approach.

BEHAVIORAL CHARACTERISTICS

18. Integrated Business Planning is a team-based process demonstrating effective group dynamics, breadth of organizational involvement, preparation and participation, open sharing, commitment, and accountability.

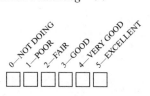

a. <u>Leadership</u>

Leadership for this management style is paramount and will determine its success. Leadership and commitment are displayed throughout the process.

b. <u>Collective Behavioral Responsibility</u>

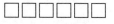

A team-based style drives a business rather than functional perspective. Collective decision making and problem solving are stated objectives. Common goals are established and functional barriers are broken down, enabling sharing and discussion of multiple views to enable achievement of consensus.

c. <u>Accountability</u>

Performance is measured and accountability is clearly set out in policy. Active participation in the planning process ensures participants have a clear understanding of the commitments made and the resulting expectations.

d. <u>Empowerment</u>

The framework of the process empowers decision making. The process drives broad-based and increased involvement in business management with decision taking at the appropriate level in the process and issues elevated by exception. Feedback to all involved in the process is routine.

e. <u>Preparation</u>

Preparation is crucial to enable effective review and data-driven decision making. Data are available in advance of each review to facilitate this. There are no surprises.

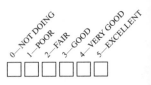

19. The culture of Integrated Business Planning is one of trust in the process, managing with an integrated set of numbers, and generation of management information to enable effective decision taking.

a. Integrated Set of Data

The process is enabled and driven by an integrated set of data and supported by a database with fast and effective data transfer, manipulation, and presentation.

b. Respect and Trust

Participants behave with integrity, and hidden agendas have been eliminated. There is trust in the process, the validity of the data, the plans, and the underlying assumptions; decisions originating from prior reviews in the process are respected.

c. Top-Down Behavior

Top-down behaviors that drive the distortion of numbers have been eliminated. Stretch goals are only included in projections to the extent that plans are in place to meet them and are underpinned by assumptions. The negative influences of financial period ends, to drive short-term actions that are inappropriate for the long-term health of the business, have been minimized.

d. <u>Supporting Processes</u>

The Integrated Business Planning process is supported in the shorter term by robust daily/weekly processes and defined authority levels to make decisions. This enables the senior team to focus further ahead, trusting that short-term exceptions will be flagged for their attention as they arise.

e. <u>Process Improvement</u>

There is an ongoing critique of the process in the drive for excellence. This includes a thirst for learning and a willingness to benchmark against best practice.

BUSINESS PERFORMANCE MEASURES

The expected suite of business performance measures will include the following core measures, supplemented by business specific measures dependent on strategy focus.

The standard for each measure will be either upper-quartile performance, a minimum standard of 99.5 percent, or attainment of business plan (as indicated). This measure demonstrates continuous performance improvement.

1. <u>Sales Revenue</u>
   Sales revenue attainment of business plan
   Measurement standard: Plan attainment
2. <u>Operating Profit</u>
   Operating profit attainment of business plan and as a benchmark against industry standards
   Measurement standard: (a) Plan attainment; (b) upper-quartile performance of "Return on Sales"
3. <u>Return on Net Assets</u>
   Ratio of operating profit to the net trading assets as attainment of

business plan and as a benchmark against industry standards. Measurement standard: (a) Plan attainment; (b) upper-quartile performance of RONA/ROCE (as preferred)

4. Cash

Operating cash flow attainment of the business plan
Measurement standard: Plan attainment

5. Customer OTIF to Request

On-Time-In-Full (OTIF) against request is measured against a standard established in the business strategy.

Measurement standard: (a) Attainment of strategy; (b) upper-quartile performance

5

MANAGING PRODUCTS AND SERVICES

PURPOSE

To ensure that the business plan requirement for Product and Services sales is achieved by the management of product portfolios and life-cycles. To create competitive advantage through upper-quartile performance.

Chapter Content

Strategy
Integration
Product Management and Marketing
Managing and Controlling Projects and Programs
Managing Resources
Managing Technology and Innovation
Team-Based Project Management and Concurrency
Performance Measurement
Behavioral Characteristics
BUSINESS PERFORMANCE MEASURES

STRATEGY

1. The product and service strategy supports the market strategy and includes the technology strategy. It drives the Product Management process.

a. Congruence with Business Strategy

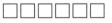

The Product Manager understands the strategic company direction and strategic objectives, and translates these into product strategy and product life-cycle tactics. Each new product and service can be related directly to at least one business strategy.

b. Congruence with Market Strategy

All product and services development can be related directly to the market strategy through the product and service strategies.

c. Competitive Analysis

The company product development process is compared at least annually to market, competition, industry standards and practices to identify upper-quartile performance and beyond.

d. Technology Strategy

The Technology Strategy identifies the core technologies and capabilities to fulfill the business strategy and defines the affordable company Research and Development and investment program.

2. Product Management directs brands, markets, segments, product groups, product life cycles, and technology deployment.

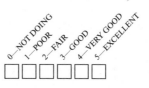

a. <u>Brand Strategy and Management</u>

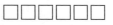

The company product and service brand(s) and their associated messages are defined and managed consistently, and in alignment with the business strategy.

b. <u>Product Groups</u>

Products with similar characteristics and requirements are identified and grouped, and the plan forward for each group is clear and consistent with the aggregate plan for the whole business.

c. <u>Product Life Cycles</u>

A process exists to monitor and forecast product life-cycle trends for each group and so plan product introduction and phase-out.

d. <u>Technology Deployment</u>

Opportunities for new and available technologies are identified, and product plans exist to lever maximum return from technology investment across the business.

INTEGRATION

3. Product and Service plans are assessed, balanced to capability, and managed through a monthly product review process. Integration with demand management, supply chain, and financial planning is ensured through an Integrated Business Planning process.

a. <u>Process Mechanism</u>

The linkage between Product and Services management and the other elements in the process is defined and made explicit.

b. Linkage to Demand Plans

The Product Management process ensures output of numbers and assumptions are aligned to the Managing Demand monthly process.

c. Linkage to Supply Chain Plans

The Product Management process ensures output of numbers and assumptions are aligned to the supply management monthly process.

d. Linkage to Financial Plans

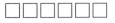

The Product Management process ensures output of numbers and assumptions are aligned to the Integrated Reconciliation and financial management monthly processes.

e. Reconciliation Management

When conflicts exist, Product Management is proactive in seeking business solutions where the proposed plan implies gaps to business plans or where risks are deemed unacceptable.

4. Processes exist to forge the operating links for day-to-day planning and execution, providing visibility and control of uncertainty, and enabling consistent and improving performance to achieve Strategic Business Objectives.

a. Product Management Defined

The Product Management role and process have been defined. The process has been mapped to ensure there is good understanding of the scope, the purpose, and the value added of each step.

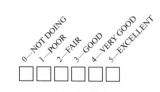

b. Interfaces with Other Processes Defined

Processes exist to accept information from, and to provide input to, other business processes and to understand and respond to them.

c. Gap Management

Performance measures identify opportunities for improvement in order to bridge the gap to Strategic Business Objectives.

d. Product Coordinator

A product coordinator has been appointed to support project and program leaders' communication with the various reviews. The Product Coordinator also keeps track of milestone adherence and any threats to product delivery and launch, and engages management to drive solutions.

PRODUCT MANAGEMENT AND MARKETING

5. **All market areas that can provide information to help create and/or modify strategies that contribute to the formulation of company targets and goals are supported by a process to penetrate and capture all relevant data.**

a. Markets, Sectors, and Channels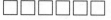

There is a process for Product Management to understand the characteristics of the chosen markets, sectors, and channels to keep product development relevant.

b. <u>Portfolio Plan</u>

The portfolio plan is a time-phased plan that defines the portfolio of current products, the additions to the portfolio through new product launches, and the removal from the portfolio through product phase-out plans. The purpose is to manage the portfolio dynamically to achieve business objectives and to close business performance gaps.

c. <u>Development Pipeline Status</u>

The number of projects at each development stage is tracked. The volume and attrition rate are consistent with the product management strategy for sustaining the business and meeting growth objectives.

d. <u>Market Share by Sector</u>

Product management are aware of market share and profitability by sector for current product groups and work to close gaps toward desired business goals.

e. <u>Competitive Analysis</u>

At least yearly, product management analyze the strengths, weaknesses, opportunities, and threats to the company's product and service offerings as driven by their Value Proposition.

f. <u>Market Analyses</u>

Ongoing market analyses provide the framework for Product Management. The analyses include the impact of product extensions and promotions, are subject to strengths, weaknesses, opportunities, and threats analysis, and continuously update the assumptions.

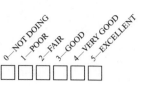

6. Techniques are employed to enable a comprehensive analysis and understanding of both customer and consumer future needs, linked to demand creation.

a. <u>Gaining Insights into Customer and Consumer Needs</u>

A Consumer insights process gains deep knowledge of end customer/consumer needs as expressed, deduced, or created to keep the product portfolio competitive and successful.

b. <u>Use of Customer Satisfaction Surveys</u>

Customer satisfaction surveys are conducted, preferably continually, to understand customer "dissatisfiers" that can be addressed through Product Management.

c. <u>Anticipating Customer/Consumer Needs</u>

Customer/Consumer insights, surveys, and analyses enable Product Management to develop product and services that anticipate and create customer needs, needs that the customer may be unaware of, or does not realize there can be a solution to. The excitement of customers/consumers that this creates is key to step change in market share.

d. <u>Link to Demand Creation</u>

A process exists to integrate new product development with demand creation to validate demand assumptions and the business case.

e. <u>Documented Customer Needs</u>

Customer needs and anticipated needs are identified, captured, and formally documented in a way that future enabling technology demands and trends can be clearly identified.

7. Portfolio management is used to manage product life cycles and the company's offerings that create ongoing excitement in the market place.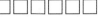

a. <u>Portfolio Management</u>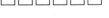

A process exists to maintain alignment of the portfolio to marketing tactics, and supply and logistics capability, in the chosen market sectors.

b. <u>Balancing the Portfolio</u>

The portfolio of products/services that are new and under development is reviewed at least quarterly to ensure an appropriate mix of high and low yielding products and high and low risk projects.

c. <u>Phase-Out/Phase-In</u>

There is a formal process to manage product phase-in/phase-out so that the business implications are optimized.

d. <u>Product Life Cycle Management</u>

A process exists to integrate the transitions of products from "new," to "mature," through to "decaying" with the rest of the business processes, and especially the links to demand and supply chain.

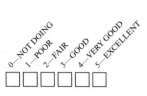

e. <u>Tactical Launch</u>

There is evidence that launch plans and timing are defined based on the latest information on the competition and opportunities.

8. There is a business-based continuous filtering
process to ensure alignment to strategy.
The process ensures correct selection,
prioritization, and resourcing of active
projects and approved proposals.

a. <u>Projects Prioritization</u>

A business filter process is ongoing and is used to filter and prioritize projects and project proposals to achieve the business needs through available resources.

b. <u>Prioritization Process Considers Competence</u>

The prioritization process includes match and availability of the skills, competencies, and capabilities of the resources available.

c. <u>Business Filter</u>

Depending on the development cycle time, there is a formal procedure specifying the frequency, decision makers, and other potential attendees. The business filter meeting has been scheduled to satisfy integration requirements.

d. <u>Project Assumptions</u>

The assumptions in the business case for individual project selection are continuously monitored, and the project will be resubmitted to the business filter upon any significant change of assumptions.

e. Justification Based on Multiple Criteria

Project justification is based on multiple business criteria, not just financial criteria. This ensures a holistic business balance in the portfolio.

9. All approved projects are contained in a formally managed New Product Master Plan, which determines and communicates the order and priority of project activity to meet the business needs.

a. New Product Master Plan

The time-phased New Product Master Plan is the formal list of all approved and resourced projects. Only projects on that list are being worked on. Stability is a desired characteristic of the New Product Master Plan, other than the natural attrition through the development pipeline. The volatility of the New Product Master Plan is tracked and shows an improving trend.

b. New Product Master Plan Balance

The New Product Master Plan is made up of projects which are business focused and that have a balance of timescale and risk.

MANAGING AND CONTROLLING PROJECTS AND PROGRAMS

10. A formal project management process exists to establish development and launch plans, provide visibility, and control execution and costs.

a. Project Planning and Control Process

All projects are planned and managed through a common formal process to ensure the best use of resources and competencies, and to achieve delivery at the required time, cost, and quality.

b. Decision Checkpoints

The project control process includes Decision Checkpoints (Gates) to review the status of the project, and progressive milestones to manage progress between decision checkpoints. Milestone plan adherence shows at least 95 percent milestones achieved on time and within cost tolerance.

c. Cost Control Process

A formal cost control process is used to ensure that projects are launched within their approved budget. This includes routine reviews, leading to corrective actions if cost is trending toward the risk contingency limits.

d. Managing the Launch

The decision to launch is taken at the launch decision point (Gate). A formal prelaunch checklist is used to minimize the risk attached to the launch.

e. Postlaunch Review

A formal postlaunch review is conducted following initial market reaction to the new product or service. This is used to drive learnings to improve the effectiveness of future development and introductions. Time-to-Volume and Time-to-Profit are tracked and show an improving trend.

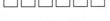

f. Ownership through to Profit

The project team supports the launch and early experiences, and a core team retains ownership until the product recovers its cost and starts generating profit.

11. The project management process is used at all levels of the company to highlight issues and barriers to success. Decisions are made in sufficient time for them to be effective.

a. Decision Escalation

Decision making has been empowered throughout the organization, and there is a formal decision escalation process to obtain the required authority.

b. Timely Decisions

Management decisions are made in a timely manner to ensure that project plans are not delayed.

c. Project Reviews

Management are engaged in decision making about the project's progress during the whole development cycle through formal review meetings.

d. Risk Management

Risk Management and Contingency Planning techniques are used to anticipate potential threats and problems and to support decision making.

12. Program Management is applied to the integration and synchronization of multiple interdependent projects.

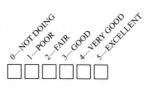

a. <u>Program Management</u>

Program Management is the concurrent management of integrated and interdependent projects that in combination deliver the required objectives.

b. <u>Program Management Process and Tools</u>

The concept of Program Management is well understood and applied to situations involving the integration and synchronization of multiple interdependent projects.

c. <u>Common Strategy and Business Plan</u>

There exists an agreed common strategy and business plan among the program partners (internal and external) regarding achieving the program objectives.

d. <u>Integrated Techniques</u>

Integrated Program Management techniques drive program deliverables through control of projects' cost and schedule deliverables. There is a program level process to command and control synchronization that involves all program partner projects.

e. <u>Service Level Agreements</u>

Formal Service Level Agreements are used to ensure synchronized and quality deliverables through the program. Key Performance Indicators validate that the Service Level Agreements are being worked to.

f. <u>Review Process</u>

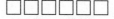

There is a monthly formal review process that includes measures and tolerances, which may then lead to an issue review meeting.

MANAGING RESOURCES

13. There is a time-phased aggregate resource allocation process, built from detailed project plans, that aligns resources to forward plans based on core competencies.

a. <u>Resource Allocation</u>

There is a process to ensure proper allocation of resources to meet the required strategic competitive position and timing.

b. <u>Load Profiles and Work Breakdown Structures</u>

Load profiles, work breakdown structures, and responsibility charts are used to develop the resource needs. Resource "planned hours" are based on demonstrated capability, and flexing/hedging levels are defined according to needs.

c. <u>Resource Management</u>

All projects in the New Product Master Plan are regularly reviewed for time-phased resource requirements. Total resource requirements are understood, and plans are in place to ensure the need will be met. Resource allocation is managed across all projects.

d. <u>Development versus Supply Needs</u>

Where there is a conflict between supply plans of current products or services and development plans, any issues that cannot be otherwise resolved are elevated to Integrated Business Planning.

14. Skills and competencies are developed to support current and future needs, in both development and delivery.

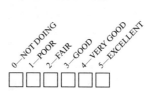

a. <u>Developing Skills and Competencies</u>

The skills and competencies required to under-take current and future needs of Product Management are understood. Plans and actions are in place to meet the need.

b. <u>Continuous Improvement</u>

Product strategy is supported by a company-wide commitment to improve continually the product development and delivery process.

c. <u>Leveraging the Extended Supply Chain</u>

The extended supply chain collaborates with their own design solutions to ensure the successful deployment of the product strategy through the utilization of end to end supply chain competencies.

d. <u>Learning from the Past</u>

Current and future product development utilizes lessons learned from the past to improve and accelerate the process facilitating the capturing of knowledge in the processes and procedures. It is sufficiently understood to be incorporated into business systems.

MANAGING TECHNOLOGY AND INNOVATION

15. The company understands the core technologies that underpin the business.

a. <u>Core Technologies</u>

The company understands and controls its core technologies that underpin the business (now and in the future) and is investing in them.

b. <u>Concept of Critical Mass</u>

Where the core technology is important to the business but the required capability is not in place, then decisions are made to develop it, buy it, delay, or change strategy.

c. <u>Extended Supply Chain and Technology</u>

The extended supply chain is recognized as a potential source of technology input. Customer and supplier partners leverage collaborative strengths, recognizing that various partners may be driving the development process at different times, according to skill and competency or business need.

16. Innovation and Knowledge Management are exploited.

a. <u>Idea Creation</u>

The nature of idea creation is understood; funding and the environment support idea creation and development aligned to the Value Proposition.

b. <u>Exploitation of New Ideas</u>

Active programs are in place to promote new ideas and innovation. Processes exist to identify, protect, and exploit ideas.

c. <u>Knowledge Management</u>

Knowledge Management is used to maintain a repository for key knowledge gained through an open idea creation and testing process.

TEAM-BASED PROJECT MANAGEMENT AND CONCURRENCY

17. The company has a Team-Based culture facilitating concurrent project design and development. This improves velocity and ability to deliver and increases right-first-time performance.

a. <u>Team-Based Project Management</u>

Team-Based Project Management is used to facilitate sharing of knowledge and activities, enabling execution of work elements in parallel to accelerate time-to-market. Self-managed team capabilities are developing.

b. <u>Extended Project Teams</u>

Multifunctional project teams may be extended to include customers and suppliers, where necessary, and external technology owners.

c. <u>Project Control</u>

Team-based project management utilizes the decision checkpoint control process to ensure formal control of development activities.

d. <u>Improving Design and Reliability</u>

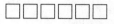

Advanced techniques are used to improve design and product reliability and to develop new product master data, specifications, and other business definitions.

e. <u>Quality and Regulatory Compliance</u>

Quality and regulatory criteria are embodied in project specifications to ensure that products and services comply with internal and external standards.

PERFORMANCE MEASUREMENT

18. A balanced set of measures exists to manage and improve processes and performance of Product and Service Management. All measures have ownership and accountability and are integrated as part of a company suite to drive business improvement.

a. Ownership and Accountability

All the product/service life-cycle partners have agreed upon a common definition for project delivery performance and related measures. Overall performance measures are visible at all points along the life-cycle chain and co-owned.

b. Reward Systems

Individual and team reward systems are designed to ensure that the whole of the product/service life-cycle chain is optimized rather than the parts.

c. Goal Driven to Strategic Business Objectives

Performance and improvements are goal driven to achieve Strategic Business Objectives.

d. Product and Services Performance Scorecards

The Key Performance Indicators are visible through scorecards and shared with design, development, and launch partners on a monthly basis, at a minimum. Trend charts are visible and show active, continuous improvement through waste elimination as well as application of root cause analysis and corrective actions.

BEHAVIORAL CHARACTERISTICS

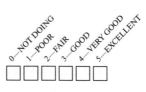

19. Management demonstrate their commitment to excellence in Product and Services Management.

a. <u>Management Commitment to Excellence</u>

Management demonstrate their commitment to excellence through allocation of resources and budget to stimulate teamwork and innovation, and through support of the empowered project/program managers.

b. <u>Logical, Timely Business Decisions</u>

Management use information to gain knowledge to support logical and timely business decisions.

c. <u>Gate Review Decisions</u>

Management demonstrably use Gate reviews to make sound, sometimes unpalatable, business decisions.

d. <u>Teams Are the Primary Vehicle for New Product and Service Delivery</u>

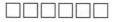

Teams are used to multiply the strength of the organization. Clearly identifiable teams are utilized as the primary means to perform development work, as opposed to individual job functions or independent work assignments.

e. <u>Empowered Development Teams</u>

Freedom and responsibility to act in alignment with product development goals and objectives are used as the basis to establish empowered development teams.

20. There is clear focus from all involved in delivering the projects to plan.

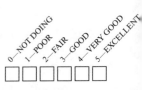

a. <u>Roles to Make Business, Not "Silos,"</u>
   <u>Successful</u>

Roles and responsibilities clearly underline working together to make the business successful.

b. <u>Product and Service Design Team Keep</u>
   <u>Projects on Track</u>

Design teams resolve issues to keep the project on track through problem solving and making timely decisions.

c. <u>Leveraging the Supply Chain</u>

Designs, drawings, specifications, bills and routings, and other business data are transmitted to the supply chain in a timely manner so that the supply chain can properly support and speed the development process.

d. <u>Importance of Velocity and Being Time</u>
   <u>Driven</u>

All involved understand and show in their behaviors that time is of the essence.

e. <u>Management Involvement</u>

Through the structured checkpoint process, management are involved early in the project to drive decisions and speed development while options are open.

f. <u>Driving the Future Organization—Evolution</u>
   <u>to "Surgeon Structure"</u>

Management progressively evolve the organization to one that is Team-Based; this provides the stepping stone for Process-Based and Matrix structures, which in turn may lead to a Surgeon Structure with its need to manage the "Incubator."

BUSINESS PERFORMANCE MEASURES

The expected suite of business performance measures will include the following core measures, supplemented by business-specific measures dependent on strategy focus.

The standard for each measure will be either upper-quartile performance, a minimum standard, or attainment of business plan (as indicated). This measure demonstrates continuous performance improvement.

1. Perfect Project Delivery

   Ninety-five percent of projects deliver completely to cost, specification, and initial volumes on time (within tolerances).

   Measurement standard: Minimum standard of 95 percent.

2. Right-First-Time Quality

   Design quality is benchmarked, and the number of launched projects that require postlaunch correction is significantly reducing.

   Measurement standard: upper-quartile performance

3. Time-to-Market

   The elapsed time between project launch and product or service availability to fulfill customer orders (including product time in the pipe-line to market) is measured and decreasing.

   Measurement standard: upper-quartile performance

4. Resource Productivity

   Key project resources are tracked and show a significant productivity improvement.

   Measurement standard: upper-quartile performance

5. Profitability Tracking

   New introductions achieve their planned performance in revenue and earnings as defined in their approved business justification.

   Measurement standard: Plan attainment

6
MANAGING DEMAND

PURPOSE

To ensure that the strategic and business plan revenue streams are achieved by managing marketing and sales activities through an integrated demand management process. To ensure that the needs of the consumers and customers are visible and understood throughout the organization.

Chapter Content

Demand Management Strategy
Integration
Category Management
Managing Channels
Customer Linkages
Demand Planning
Sales Planning and Execution
Demand Control
Performance Measurement
Behavioral Characteristics
BUSINESS PERFORMANCE MEASURES

DEMAND MANAGEMENT STRATEGY

1. The Sales and Marketing strategy supports the business strategy and drives the Demand Management activities of the company.

a. Value Proposition

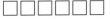

Demand strategies are congruent with the company's chosen market Value Proposition.

b. Ownership—Customer

All strategies regarding current and new customers, markets, channels, routes to market, and so on, are owned by Sales and Marketing.

c. Ownership—Product

All strategies regarding current and new products are owned by Sales and Marketing.

d. Clarity and Communication

The Sales and Marketing strategy is articulated in sufficient detail to ensure understanding by all. Strategies are communicated to all of those involved in making them happen.

2. Gaps have been identified between the strategy and present situation during the Demand Management process. Gap-closing actions are identified.

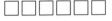

a. Gap Identification

There is a constant awareness of the strategy, and gaps are identified for the full horizon of the strategic plan. Once a gap is identified, it is articulated as to size and cause.

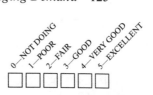

b. <u>Gap Closure by Customer, Market, Channel, and so on.</u>

Actions are planned to close gaps through activities and changes to plan with respect to customers, markets, channels, routes to market, and so on.

c. <u>Gap Closure by Product</u>

Actions are planned to close gaps through activities and changes to plan with respect to the product portfolio.

d. <u>Integration</u>

All strategy gap-closing actions are integrated into the demand planning process.

INTEGRATION

3. **Demand plans are created, assessed, and managed through a monthly Demand Review process, owned by Sales and Marketing. Integration with Product Management, Supply Chain, and Financial Planning is ensured through an Integrated Business Planning process.**

a. <u>Process Mechanism</u>

The linkage between Demand Management and the other elements in the process is defined and made explicit.

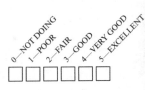

b. <u>Linkage to Product Management and Supply Chain</u>

Plans are received from Product Management as input to the monthly demand planning process. Timely output of the demand plan, as approved at the demand review, is provided monthly to supply chain as the formal request for supply.

c. <u>Linkage to Financial Plans</u>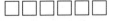

Net prices are projected out through the planning horizon. The volume plan is priced to generate the revenue plan. This revenue plan is used in all financial planning.

d. <u>Expenditure Plans</u>

Sales and Marketing expenditure plans, intended to generate demand, are reviewed during the demand planning process to ensure integration with the volume and revenue plans.

e. <u>Adjustments</u>

Demand Management is proactive in seeking business solutions where the proposed plan implies conflict with other process elements or gaps to business commitments. Adjustments made in Integrated Reconciliation or at the Management Business Review are backed up by actions from Sales and Marketing to achieve these adjusted plans.

4. Processes exist to forge the operating links required to ensure integration between Demand Management and all other operating areas, including Product Management, Supply Chain, Procurement, and Internal Supply.

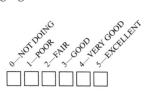

a. Product Management

Once new products and services are approved,
the demand for them is owned by Sales and Marketing and included in the overall demand plan,
which is integrated with the Product Management plans.

b. Procurement and Supply

Sales and Marketing ensure that they have visibility of reliable supply plans for all products
they are selling, whether internally or externally
sourced.

c. Supply Chain

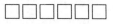

Sales and Marketing must see themselves as
being part of a supply chain and must source
whatever information they can to enable an understanding of the demands for all the steps in
that supply chain.

d. Support Functions

Sales and Marketing must ensure alignment
with corporate strategies in supporting areas
such as HR, IT, and other support functions.

CATEGORY MANAGEMENT

**5. Where the business is segmented by categories
or assortments of products, a plan exists to
maximize the profit to the company by
managing those categories and/or assortments
for or with customers and/or markets.**

a. Focus

Product and market segmentation is used to focus efforts to offer the right products and services to the right customers.

b. Strategy

A strategy exists that defines the right category characteristics that are then targeted for specific customer or market segments.

c. Assortment Planning

Product placement is optimized to drive category revenue. Merchandise planning of product promotions, seasonality, and new product launches and complementary products are used to drive category revenue.

d. Profit

Categories are optimized for product profit contribution and aggregate category profitability based on forecasted customer demand and product margin.

6. A plan for the exploitation of product and market opportunities at each local point of consumption is in place.

a. "Micro" Marketing

Detailed category assortments are developed based on local customer-specific traits such as demographic or geographic needs, and assumptions are documented as to why these specific traits were developed.

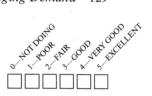

b. <u>Demand Plans</u>

Detailed category demand plans are used as an input to the aggregate demand plans for the company.

c. <u>Category Plans</u>

Detailed market plans exist to implement the assumptions underlying the demand plan for each category. These plans are integrated with the day-to-day and month-to-month activities of the Sales and Marketing teams.

MANAGING CHANNELS

7. Different channels are formally recognized and strategies developed.

a. <u>Characteristics</u>

The characteristics of the channels are understood. The planning process differentiates the channels, and actions throughout are segregated, where relevant, into these channels.

b. <u>Expectations</u>

The customer expectations in each channel are measured and understood. Responsiveness is deliberately aligned with those expectations.

c. <u>Channel Plans</u>

Detailed market plans exist to implement the assumptions underlying the demand plan for each channel. This plan is integrated with the day-to-day and month-to-month activities of the Sales and Marketing teams. The assumptions underlying the plans are measured to ensure their validity and drive actions.

d. <u>Demand Plans</u>

Channel demand plans are used as input to the aggregate demand plans for the company.

CUSTOMER LINKAGES

8. There is an understanding of the advantages of Customer Relationship Management for managing and anticipating customer requirements and expectations.

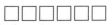

a. <u>Formal Documented Process</u>

An efficient, effective process exists to manage the interaction with customers. Links are established between qualitative measures of customer understanding and quantitative business measures.

b. <u>Goals and Benefits</u>

Benefits associated with the Customer Relationship Management process can be demonstrated in terms of customer acquisition, retention, and loyalty, and justified through a Return On Investment evaluation. The benefits are aligned with the company's Value Proposition.

c. <u>Valued Customers</u>

The company can demonstrate commitment to listening to, studying, or measuring the value of their customers to the organization. The company knows its customers and potential customers.

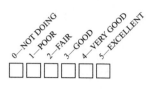

d. <u>Differentiation and One-to-One Marketing</u>

Customers are differentiated in terms of value to the organization and in terms of their requirements and needs. Sales and Marketing strategies, tactics, and planning are adjusted based on this differentiation. The process provides the organization with the ability to customize its marketing to each individual customer's needs.

e. <u>Measurement</u>

Customers' feelings, attitudes, complaints, habits, behaviors, and financial value to the company are measured, tracked, and linked. Business efforts are adjusted based on customer intelligence.

9. Collaboration with customers is being developed: business planning, demand planning, operational planning and execution, and performance measurement are embraced.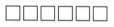

a. <u>Joint Strategy</u>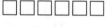

Collaborative planning is seen as a way of forming stronger strategic alliances, not only as a way of improving transactional effectiveness. Joint benefits from collaborative planning are shared between the two parties.

b. <u>Collaborative Replenishment</u>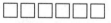

Collaborative replenishment processes are established with the purpose of creating mutual business benefits and competitive advantage for both parties. The means of exchanging data have been simplified as far as possible.

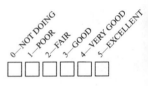

c. Pull

There is the ambition of establishing pull to customer demand with the next steps of the supply chain so that demand at each step is synchronized. Sales actively pursue this goal with customers in joint activities with the supply chain.

d. Organizational Relationship

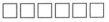

Traditional single point of contact has been replaced by multiple-point contacts, and the roles in this relationship are clearly defined.

e. Performance Measures

Collaborative performance measure definitions are shared, balanced, and aligned. Root Cause Analysis is a joint effort between the enterprises.

DEMAND PLANNING

10. An unconstrained demand plan exists that is used as the sole source of demand plans for all business processes.

a. Ownership

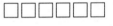

The ownership for the demand plan is in Sales and Marketing, and no other demand plans or forecasts exist. Forecast accuracy is measured to accountability level, and bias has been eliminated.

b. Demand Plan Accuracy

Demand plan accuracy is measured to accountability level, and bias has been eliminated.

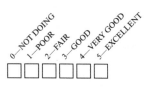

c. <u>Unconstrained Demand</u>

Any imbalance between the unconstrained and constrained demand plan should be resolved through a formal process, the final output of which is used in all business processes.

d. <u>Assumptions</u>

Sales and Marketing assumptions underpin the demand plan and are fully documented, time phased, and owned. The effects of demand levers are understood and effectively managed by both Sales and Marketing.

e. <u>Frequency of Update</u>

The demand plan is reviewed for updates or changes on at least a monthly basis. If changes occur between reviews then they are communicated to the planning processes that need to know.

f. <u>Horizon and Detail</u>

The horizon and level of detail are consistent with the Integrated Business Planning process, and ownership is consistent across the entire horizon.

g. <u>Time Fences/Decision Points</u>

Time fences/decision points are agreed upon, and their implications are known and understood, including the effect on the level of detail required from the demand plan. Updates to the demand plan are managed and made at any time without regard to the time zone that is affected.

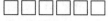

11. **A process exists to ensure that multiple views of market and customer demands are obtained. These include customer-based views and market-based views.**

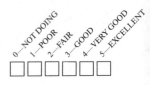

a. Product Management Input

Product Managers (or equivalent) regularly review the life cycles of their existing products, assessing their impact on the projected volumes. Seasonality is assessed, and planned promotions are taken into account.

b. Marketing Input

There is a market perspective taken of demand. This takes into account brand plans, all marketing activities (both product and market specific), promotions, and activities aimed at key opinion leaders, as well as similar activities expected from the competition. Relevant market-related measures are also tracked, such as market penetration, share, size, share of voice, and so on.

c. Sales Input

There is a formal process for capturing and consolidating information from the field that is relevant to the demand planning process. The sales force understands the value of this input and actively seeks relevant news, particularly in its interaction with customers.

d. Customer Input

Information is gathered with regard to customers' business plans and operational plans. Key Account Managers, or people in similar functions, understand their role in collecting this type of information. Before incorporating any customer inputs into the demand plan there is a process for analyzing, understanding, and taking internal ownership for that demand.

e. <u>External Influences</u>

Information is gathered and used regarding industry trends, economic conditions, competitor activity, and other extrinsic factors.

f. <u>Statistical Forecasting Input</u>

Statistical forecasting is used to provide a projected base line. Statistical projections are done based on cleansed history. Statistical models and the effect of statistical forecasting parameters are understood. The statistical forecast is one of the multiple view inputs used in the development of the final demand plan.

12. A plan exists for how the volume/revenue gaps from the demand plan to the business plan and targets are to be closed from existing and new products, customers, and markets.

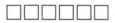

a. <u>Change Understood</u>

The underlying change in assumptions and the conditions that caused the gap are identified and understood.

b. <u>Authority Level</u>

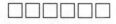

The authority for making decisions at the Demand Review level is clear. Only decisions that cannot be made at this level are escalated.

c. <u>Opportunities</u>

Opportunities (upsides) on volume and revenue numbers not included in the current plan have been identified for possible exploitation.

d. <u>Vulnerabilities</u>

Vulnerabilities (downsides) on volume and revenue numbers included in the current plan have been clearly identified, and defense countermeasures have been put in place to mitigate the risk.

e. <u>Making Recommendations</u>

Gaps are escalated from the Demand Review with gap-closing recommendations. When possible, multiple options are supplied to allow for effective scenario planning. The opportunities are used as a source for gap-closing actions.

13. The role of Demand Planning Manager has been established. This is an analysis and facilitation role for the demand planning process.

a. <u>Role Ownership</u>

The role of the Demand Planning Manager is seen by Sales and Marketing as being theirs, reporting within that organization.

b. <u>Ownership of the Demand Plan</u>

While the demand plan is owned by Sales and Marketing, the Demand Planning Manager is responsible for managing the data.

c. <u>Demand Planning Review Meetings</u>

The Demand Planning Manager facilitates the monthly Demand Review, performing this service for the executive owner of the Demand Plan.

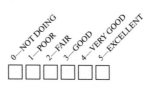

d. Communication

Sales and Marketing people communicate with the Demand Planning Manager on a regular basis and when changes occur that will affect the demand plan. The Demand Planning Manager liaises with the Supply Planner and the Product Coordinator on an ongoing basis.

e. Monitoring and Performance Analysis

The Demand Planning Manager is continuously monitoring performance to the demand plan and facilitating the analysis and understanding of variations to the demand plan.

SALES PLANNING AND EXECUTION

14. A formal set of short-term and long-term sales plans exist to manage the direction and activities of the sales force.

a. Integration with Marketing

Sales plans are integrated in terms of volume and value with the marketing and/or brand plans. The assumptions (including competitor activity) that support these plans are documented and reviewed.

b. Detailed Sales Plan

Detailed sales plans exist to implement or countermeasure the assumptions underlying the demand plan. These plans are integrated with the day-to-day and month-to-month activities of the Sales teams, including account management, call cycles, and follow-up activity.

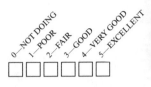

c. <u>Buildup</u>

Sales plans, built up by significant customer, sales channel, and territorial area, support the delivery of the company's marketing and business plans. The accuracy of this sales plan is measured.

d. <u>Sales Plan and Constrained Demand Plan</u>

The sales plan is aligned with the constrained demand plan.

e. <u>Sales Force Performance</u>

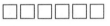

The delivery of the plans by customer, sales channel, and territorial area is measured and tracked so that the performance of the sales force can be understood and improved.

15. Sales objectives and processes are in place to drive sales force activity in line with the sales plan.

a. <u>Formal Sales Process</u>

A formal process is defined and followed. The process outlines the stages and steps involved in the selling process and the criteria to move to the next activity. Bid/no bid and other qualification points are defined.

b. <u>Sales Force Activity</u>

Sales force activity key performance indicators, targets, incentives, and bonuses are aligned with the demand plan to ensure integration and avoid bias.

c. <u>Monitoring</u>

A formal monitoring system is in place to ensure that any variance from target is promptly identified and addressed.

d. <u>Constraints</u>

Constraints in the execution of the sales plan are related back to their impact on the demand plan.

DEMAND CONTROL

16. A process exists to prioritize and manage demand when demand is greater than the supply plan.

a. <u>Managing Supply to Match Demand</u>

Formal monthly Supply Reviews are undertaken to manage capability to meet unconstrained demand. Supply priorities are set by the demand team to leverage demand with the greatest need. There is a constant process to ensure that this is current and that the flexibility to respond to demand changes is being improved.

b. <u>Time Fences and Decision Points</u>

The ability of the supply chain to respond economically is understood, and decisions regarding requests for changes to the supply plan are managed accordingly.

c. <u>Decision-Making Authority</u>

When actual demand exceeds planned supply, decisions are escalated as a function of the magnitude of the impact on profitability and/or commercial strategy. This process is coordinated and designed to maximize the business opportunity.

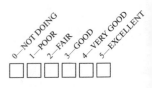

d. <u>Managing Demand to Match Supply</u>

Monthly unconstrained demand plans are aligned to available supply. Constrained demand plans are created to match the available supply. There is an ongoing review of these situations between monthly reviews.

e. <u>Constant Synchronization</u>

Formal processes have been documented with the roles, responsibilities, and review time periods for aligning and synchronizing demand with supply.

17. Order promising is a managed process. Customer deliveries are only promised against planned supply capabilities. There is a process for managing key or constrained capabilities prior to order entry.

a. <u>Delivery Targets</u>

There are clearly defined targets for product availability and delivery lead times. Variances from target are periodically reviewed and corrective actions undertaken.

b. <u>Available to Capability or Promise</u>

Available to capability or available to promise is used in a way that maximizes the use of capacity and/or inventory for promising customers delivery against the formal supply plan.

c. <u>Realistic Delivery</u>

Where the ordering pattern is different from the planned demand time phasing, valid promises are given to the customers that reflect a realistic ability to deliver. Customers are informed in the event of changed delivery commitments.

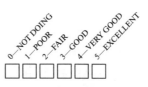

d. <u>Risk</u>

A process is in place to ensure that order promising and delivering is linked to adequate credit control and other risk procedures.

18. A process exists to reconcile incoming orders to the forecast so that the integrity of the demand plans can be sustained.

a. <u>Abnormal Demand Identification</u>

There are mechanisms in place to identify unforecast demand as early as possible. The criteria for what constitutes Abnormal Demand are clear and understood by the sales force and customer order entry representatives.

b. <u>Managing Abnormal Demand</u>

There is a formal process for resolving abnormal demand in a way that balances business objectives, commercial strategy, and immediate competitive priorities.

c. <u>Recording Abnormal Demand</u>

Abnormal Demand is flagged in the demand database so it can be filtered out for demand planning purposes. The reasons behind abnormal demand are recorded and periodically analyzed for the purpose of better understanding market dynamics, and to proactively reduce causes of abnormal demand.

d. <u>Forecast Consumption</u>

Forecast consumption is understood and is a managed process, undertaken routinely for all forecast demand.

e. Forecast Review

There is a constant process in place reviewing under- and over-forecast conditions to increase visibility of changes in demand. Changes to forecast are only made where known events have altered the assumptions supporting the demand plan.

f. Forecast Roll

There is a formal process for managing unconsumed forecast at the end of each forecasting period.

19. The role of the Demand Control Manager has been established.

a. Role

The role has been established to manage the issues in the short-term demand. This involves the identification and resolution of abnormal demand, managing available to promise, and monitoring forecast consumption. They participate in a weekly demand/supply review process.

b. Position in the Supply Chain

The Demand Control Manager operates at the point in the supply chain where independent demand is received.

c. Communication

The Demand Control Manager communicates with demand planning, supply, and finance on a regular basis and when changes occur that will affect the demand plan.

PERFORMANCE MEASUREMENT

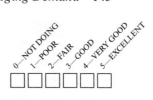

20. A balanced set of measures exists to manage and improve processes and performance in managing demand. All measures have ownership and accountability and are integrated as part of a company suite to drive business improvement.

a. <u>Balanced Set</u>

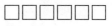

There is a balanced set of performance measures, comprising the areas of forecasting, planning, execution, and deliverables. There is also a balance between those measures and other measures of financial, operational, customer, consumer, and employee performance.

b. <u>Integrated Suite</u>

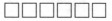

Performance measures and reward systems have been reviewed for fit with other company measures, and conflicts and redundancies have been eliminated.

BEHAVIORAL CHARACTERISTICS

21. Behaviors support the meeting of customer expectations through the business as a whole, rather than the individual functions.

a. <u>Education and Training</u>

All employees understand their role in meeting customer expectations. The relevant education and training have been provided to ensure employees' understanding and support of the process in place to ensure customer satisfaction.

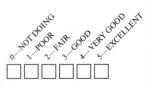

b. <u>Team-Based Activity</u>

Multifunctional team activity focused on optimizing customer satisfaction is well established.

c. <u>No End-of-Month "Push"</u>

There is no artificial end-of-month "push" to increase invoicing and reduce end-of-month inventories at the expense of the next step in the supply chain.

d. <u>Trade Push</u>

There is no pushing of product into the next step in the supply chain to improve short-term results.

e. <u>Performance Measures</u>

Performance measures and feedback systems are effective in recognizing and rewarding appropriate behaviors.

22. There is trust in the numbers that make up the plans and in people's ability to execute these plans.

a. <u>Trust</u>

There is a common, agreed upon, and shared demand plan for all functions within the company, and complete trust in the quality of those demand plans can be demonstrated by every function within the organization.

b. <u>Belief in Behavior</u>

Sales and Marketing believe that being realistic and honest about their plans, as well as being proactive in making changes to the plan, is essential to delivery of the plan.

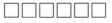

c. <u>Changing Numbers</u>

No changes are made to the numbers in the plan unless the underlying assumptions have been changed. Changes in assumptions are formally agreed upon, documented, and measured.

d. <u>Work the Plan</u>

There is a culture of planning the work and working to the plan.

e. <u>Silence Is Approval</u>

People operate on the principle of communicating anticipated issues early and recognize that, in the absence of issues and communications, silence means approval.

BUSINESS PERFORMANCE MEASURES

The expected suite of business performance measures will include the following core measures, supplemented by business-specific measures dependent on strategy focus.

The standard for each measure will be either upper-quartile performance, a minimum standard of 99.5 percent, or attainment of business plan (as indicated). This measure demonstrates continuous performance improvement.

1. <u>Aggregate Demand Plan Performance</u>
   Attainment of the demand plan approved through the Integrated Business Planning process.
   Measurement standard: Plan attainment
2. <u>Margin</u>
   Gross margins of order intake meet the gross margin expectations of the sales plan.
   Measurement standard: Plan attainment

3. Sales Contribution

    Net sales value achieved less marketing costs and sales costs measured by Marketing product group and category. Contribution achievement as a percentage of net sales price.

    Measurement standard: Plan attainment

4. Market Share

    Market share is measured by product group or category and meets the business plan ambition.

    Measurement standard: Plan attainment

5. Customer Satisfaction

    On-time delivery to request: On-Time-In-Full (OTIF) is measured and is improving.

    Measurement standard: (a) Attainment of strategy; (b) upper-quartile performance

7

MANAGING THE SUPPLY CHAIN

PURPOSE

To build an increasingly responsive supply chain that plans, integrates, links, and shapes the supply planning and execution processes to deliver competitive advantage through upper-quartile performance.

Chapter Content

Supply Chain Strategy
Integration
Supply Chain Management
Supply Chain Planning
Distribution and Logistics
Data Sharing
Supply Chain Effectiveness
Trading Partner Financial Integration
Performance Measurement
Behavioral Characteristics
BUSINESS PERFORMANCE MEASURES

SUPPLY CHAIN STRATEGY

1. **The Supply Chain strategy supports the marketing and operations strategies and drives the supply chain planning and execution. Upper-quartile performance for the extended supply chain is understood. Vision and ambition is clearly articulated and the scope of activity defined.**

a. <u>Marketing Strategy</u>

The marketing strategy defines the required supply chain flexibility and service requirements, including where differentiated service and/or supply is required. The supply chain has conducted a segmentation exercise based on that strategy.

b. <u>Supply Strategy</u>

The business has decided which supply strategies to utilize as a result of a segmentation process.

c. <u>Logistics Strategy</u>

The logistics strategy defines stocking levels, distribution, warehouses, direct ship, and transportation based on the segmentation process.

d. <u>Segmented Supply Chain</u>

Using the segmentation information, customer and product service levels are established for supply chain planning and execution goals. Different supply chains are used to provide differentiated service and/or supply based on the segmentation process.

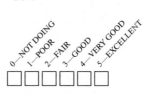

e. Supply Chain Innovation

The process of strategy review includes a blank sheet approach on how the supply chain should be operated so as to search out ways of innovating to gain competitive advantage.

f. Scope

The scope of activity for Extended Supply Chain Management, to deliver upper-quartile performance, has been specified.

2. The Extended Supply Chain is designed to optimize service, inventory, capacity, and costs.

a. Total Cost

Total cost rather than individual step costs and goals are used to determine how each step or link in the internal and external supply chain will operate to optimize the extended supply chain.

b. Demand Pull and Supply Push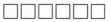

Concepts such as "demand pull" and "supply push" are understood and appropriately embedded in the supply chain design.

c. Quick Response and Continuous Replenishment

There is a process and a plan to reduce batch-processing quantities (lot sizes) with customers, suppliers, and all internal process steps. "Replace what is sold," quick response, and continuous replenishment are being pursued through the distribution network.

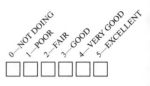

d. Lead Times and Service Times

Lead Times and Service Times are considered important, and plans exist to reduce these at every step of the supply chain.

e. Synchronization Leveling

There is a continuous process in place to drive synchronization across the supply chain, and the rhythm (Takt Time) of the consumption demand-pull is "heard" and understood throughout the supply chain.

INTEGRATION

3. Supply Chain capability and flexibility are modeled, measured, and managed through a monthly supply review process. Integration with product management, demand, supply points, and financial planning is ensured through an Integrated Business Planning process.

a. Process Mechanism

The linkage between Supply Chain Management and other elements in the Integrated Business Planning process is defined and made explicit.

b. Linkage to Product Management and Demand

Plans are received from Product Management and Demand Management as "requirements" to the monthly supply planning process. Integrated supply plans are created, recognizing capability and flexibility within the extended supply chain.

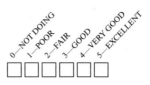

c. <u>Linkage within the Supply Chain</u>

Input is received from internal supply and external sourcing identifying capability and flexibility. Plans developed for the extended supply chain direct planning for internal supply and external sourcing.

d. <u>Linkage to Financial Planning</u>

Evaluated supply chain plans and assumptions provide visibility to financial planning on activity level, cost, and inventory and capital investment implications. The scope is the corporate supply chain and not just the parts, countries, or operating units. The financial planning process utilizes the latest supply chain plans including planned cost reduction and improvement actions.

e. <u>Reconciliation Management</u>

Supply management is proactive in seeking business solutions where the proposed plan implies constraint on product management or demand plans, gaps to business commitments, or where risks are deemed unacceptable. Adjustments made in integrated reconciliation or at the management business review are incorporated within revised supply plans.

4. Processes exist that forge the supply chain links required for day-to-day execution providing visibility and control of uncertainty. They enable consistent and improving performance to achieve strategic business objectives.

a. <u>Events and Sales and Marketing Initiatives</u>

There is clear and timely visibility of market-place events that will change demand timing, mix, and/or volumes. Sales and Marketing initiatives are formally communicated to demand and supply planners with sufficient lead time to enable valid plans.

b. <u>Information Sharing</u>

Visibility of daily supply chain activity information is shared throughout the extended supply chain.

c. <u>Collaborative Alerts</u>

Trading partners have collaboratively determined exception alerts, which generate action messages. These alerts and action messages are sent to responsible functions of the supply chain for resolution in a timely manner.

d. <u>Supply Chain Step Integration Points</u>

Integration checkpoints have been determined through collaborative planning, which are documented in collaborative arrangements to validate that new or changed plans are on track from the supply chain perspective.

e. <u>Linkage to Supply Points</u>   ☐☐☐☐☐☐

There is a formal linkage through plans and systems between the supply chain and individual supply points in the supply chain.

SUPPLY CHAIN MANAGEMENT

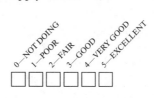

5. The supply chain is managed as a whole, consistent with the Integrated Business Planning direction.

a. Integration and Optimization

The supply chain demand plans and supply capability are integrated and optimized for use and visibility for the extended supply chain.

b. Prioritization

Priority decisions are made considering the impact on the entire supply chain, its customers, and the affected products. These are effectively communicated through the supply chain.

c. Trading Partner Collaboration

Trading partners communicate and collaborate on supply issues that may result in constrained forecasts of demand, new product constraints, and new product launch adjustments in a timely manner.

d. Product Management

Product management project activities and milestones are integrated with the Master Supply Plan at the agreed stage checkpoints.

6. Service level agreements exist between all the steps in the supply chain to support true collaboration. The supply chain is managed to these agreements.

a. Service Level Agreements

Interstep links are based on long-term partnership agreements formalized through properly structured Service Level Agreements and Joint Business Plans.

b. <u>Inventory Investment Levels</u>

Joint agreements exist on inventory stocking levels and locations.

c. <u>Improvement and Resolution of Conflict</u>

Collaborative goals and processes are established for continuous improvement and how to resolve any conflict.

d. <u>Supply Chain Time Fences</u>

Time fence parameters have been defined for coordination and acceptable execution of change for all stages.

SUPPLY CHAIN PLANNING

7. The planning processes effectively manage
and control multiple supply points to optimize
the supply chain, rather than any individual
supply point.

a. <u>Inventory and Service Levels</u>

Inventory and service levels are monitored and managed through integrated material, supplier, and resource planning and control along the supply chain.

b. <u>Extended Planning</u>

The concepts of requirements planning (using dependent demand) are employed to manage an integrated planning process from end to end of the supply chain. This will include Distribution Resource Planning, Logistics Planning, Production Planning, and Supplier Planning.

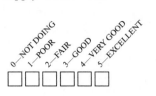

c. <u>Resource Management</u>

Key resources that affect the ability of the supply chain to perform have been identified and are managed in the planning process. The supply chain planning process plans the use of capacity and capability against these resources for the entire planning horizon based on demonstrated performance concepts.

d. <u>Integrated Planning Processes</u>

The planning processes of the extended supply chain are integrated so that all the aspects of inventory levels, lead times, and order quantities have been formalized within the planning system.

e. <u>Schedule Adherence (On Time in Full)</u>

Suppliers, all supply points, and receiving and shipping points demonstrate adherence to the supply plan time, quantity and quality at a minimum 99.5 percent.

8. Supply chain modeling techniques are used to optimize the extended supply chain.

a. <u>Supply Chain Optimization</u>

Advanced Planning System techniques are used to optimize and balance the supply chain using the rules established by the supply chain design.

b. <u>What-if Scenarios</u>

What-if scenarios are used to help determine the ability to satisfy customer demand for product delivery achieving planned total cost and investment.

c. <u>Options</u>

Multiple options are used to determine how to satisfy customer demand in the most cost-efficient and time-sensitive manner.

d. <u>Product Delivery Options</u>

Product delivery options are assessed to determine shipping priorities based on customer need by customer locations.

9. There is an Inventory Control process in place that maintains accurate inventory records throughout the supply chain.

a. <u>Inventory Management</u>

There is a clear understanding of Inventory Management practices for all necessary inventory points in the supply chain with accountability for accuracy identified through policy.

b. <u>Process Control</u>

Process Control is maintained through a formal cycle counting process that ensures reconciliation, root cause analysis, and corrective actions.

c. <u>Accuracy</u>

Inventory accuracy is measured and achieves a minimum standard of 99.5 percent.

DISTRIBUTION AND LOGISTICS

10. Distribution and logistics plans are integrated with the aggregate- and detail-level supply chain plans.

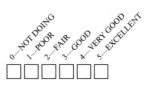

a. <u>Distribution and Integrated Business Planning</u>

Mid- to long-term distribution and logistics resource plans are based on the supply chain Integrated Business plan numbers for new product launches, demand, and replenishment of supply.

b. <u>Logistics Coordination</u>

A logistics operations coordination process is perpetually managed in order to ensure a balance of stability and responsiveness. The resource deployment plan is reconciled monthly with the monthly aggregate logistics supply plan resulting from the Integrated Business Planning process.

c. <u>Integration of Distribution and Logistics</u>

All logistics, warehousing, distribution, and transportation requirements are derived from the formal supply chain plans. Inventory management decisions at the warehouse level are integrated into demand and supply planning numbers.

d. <u>Logistics Planning</u>

There is a requirements planning process that maintains valid daily distribution schedules, along with control processes that communicate priorities through the warehouse schedules, supplier schedules, and/or pull trigger mechanisms. Inbound and outbound logistics processes are integrated within the supply chain using Distribution Resource Planning principles and tools to assure availability and service.

e. <u>Warehouse Management</u>

The warehouse management system is integrated with distribution resource planning, supporting control and management of picking, stocking, space management, and orderliness.

11. The delivery process is a key requirement in achieving perfect order fulfillment and availability for use.

a. <u>Delivery from the Supply Chain</u>

Delivery is seen as an integrated key competency, and this is reflected in the attention, standards, and budget afforded to distribution and logistics.

b. <u>Distribution Networks</u>

Where product is delivered via a distribution network, Distribution Resource Planning is employed as the process for planning and control.

c. <u>Transportation Optimization</u>

Transportation optimization techniques are utilized to facilitate full truckloads and containers for inbound and outbound, including backhauls.

d. <u>Distribution Center Optimization</u>

Distribution center optimization techniques are utilized, including cross-docking and picking linearity.

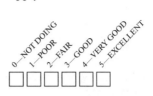

e. <u>Transportation Routing Optimization</u>

Transportation routing optimization techniques are used to determine the most cost-effective modes of delivery, including sea, air, rail, and ground. Routing schedules are optimized, based on lead time considerations ensuring customer service levels are attained.

DATA SHARING

12. There is a formal process for the sharing and setting of data parameters that support integrated and collaborative planning with all trading partners.

a. <u>Service Level Agreements</u>

Supply chain collaborative agreements have formal policy statements defining data sharing models, sources of data, methods of data transmission, and confidentiality rules.

b. <u>Data Sharing Model</u>

Trading partners jointly agree on what data are shared, how the data are to be shared, when the data are shared, and with whom the data are shared.

c. <u>Data Structure and Nomenclature</u>

Data formats are predefined, and documentation for data definition is available and understood.

d. Understanding Reconciliation

d. Minimal Reconciliation

Action messages and tolerances for supply chain processing have been defined by the trading partners. The supply chain is managed by exception and allows normal processing to flow through automatically. Action message text has been defined with the required data and recipients.

e. Transmission of Data

Data process flows are maintained and transmission/data format models conform to agreed definitions and industry guidelines.

13. Data (including Rules) used to drive the supply chain are understood, accurate, and owned. These data are subject to stringent change control and security safeguards.

a. Understanding

Users and owners of data have been educated and trained on their purpose and impact on the business.

b. Ownership

Ownership and accountability for all data have been clearly established.

c. Change Control Process

There is a change control process in place that covers the identification of changes and additions through to approval and implementation of those changes.

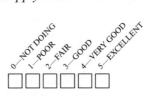

d. Data Integrity

An auditing process exists that verifies accuracy of data used across the supply chain; the measure shows that accuracy is being maintained at a minimum of 99.5 percent.

e. Obsolete Data Removal

There is an information management procedure that archives obsolete data.

SUPPLY CHAIN EFFECTIVENESS

14. Non-value-adding steps in the supply chain have been minimized. There is a continuous improvement process in place to identify activity for further elimination or optimization.

a. Supply Chain Agility

The requirement for agility is understood and established in line with the supply chain strategy. Improvements in agility can be demonstrated.

b. Supply Chain Costs

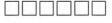

Requirements for cost reduction along the supply chain are understood and established in line with supply chain strategy. Improvements in costs along the supply chain can be demonstrated.

c. Value Stream Mapping

Value Stream Mapping is used to understand and optimize activities along the length of the supply chain and not just within each step. There is an agreed definition of value among trading partners in the supply chain.

d. Activity-Based Management

Cost drivers in the supply chain are understood and agreed upon. There is a process for identifying value-adding and non-value-adding activity and removing waste. These drivers are managed and are an integral part of business decision making in the supply chain.

e. Velocity Ratio is Measured

Velocity Ratio is measured for the whole supply chain. Velocity improvements can be demonstrated and are reflected in reduced planning lead times.

15. Lean distribution and logistics techniques are employed to improve efficiency.

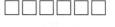

a. Warehousing

Warehouse layout is designed to reduce "touch," optimize pick, and reduce movement and other sources of waste. Appropriate automation, such as sortation systems, is employed to eliminate consolidation errors.

b. Replenishment

Quick response and continuous replenishment where appropriate are used to maintain service and stock levels through the distribution network replacing what is sold.

c. Transportation

Transportation process flows have been defined to reduce wait times, excessive transit times, and excessive distance.

d. Collaborative Transportation

Collaborative and third-party transportation techniques that leverage collaboration between carrier companies are used to help reduce costs by taking advantage of load sharing and carrier sharing. Return journeys and triangulation are regularly used to reduce cost.

TRADING PARTNER FINANCIAL INTEGRATION

16. **There is an adequate understanding of the margins, costs, and investments in the supply chain. There is a process in place to optimize the rewards versus costs along the chain.**

a. Transparency of Suppliers

There is a clear understanding of the profit and cost structures and drivers of our key suppliers and their key suppliers.

b. Transparency with Customers

There is a clear understanding of the supply chain cost structures and drivers of our key customers and their customers.

c. What-if Analysis

A process exists to analyze scenarios in the extended enterprise profits and costs to drive improvement priorities.

d. Rewards

Incentives are in place to encourage optimal cost performance of the extended supply chain.

PERFORMANCE MEASUREMENT

17. A balanced set of measures exists to manage and improve processes and performance in the supply chain. All measures have ownership and accountability and are integrated as part of a company suite to drive business improvement.

a. Balanced Set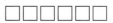

There is a balance of measures (financial, operational, external) used within the supply chain. The trading partners understand that the overall supply chain delivery performance is the product of the performance of each step.

b. Integrated Suite

Conflict between measures has been minimized through the setting of strategic priorities. Measures that promote extended supply chain thinking rather than functional behaviors are employed.

c. Ownership and Accountability

All the partners in the extended supply chain have agreed upon a common definition for service level measurement and related measures. Overall supply chain service performance measures are visible at all supply points and are co-owned.

d. Goal Driven to Strategic Business Objectives

Individuals and teams in the supply chain have clear goals and targets linked to the strategic objectives of the business. Reward systems are designed to ensure that the whole of the extended supply chain is optimized rather than the parts.

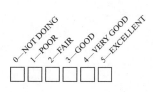

e. <u>Supply Chain Performance Scorecards</u>

The key performance indicators are visible through agreed scorecards and are shared with all supply chain partners on at least a monthly basis. Trend charts are visible and show continuous improvement through application of root cause analysis and corrective actions.

BEHAVIORAL CHARACTERISTICS

18. Interentity payment and profit processes encourage appropriate supply chain behavior.

a. <u>Cost Centers</u>

Internal supply chain steps are considered cost centers in the supply chain. Where artificial profit is used as an incentive between internal steps in the supply chain it is not a barrier to optimization.

b. <u>Decisions Are Made Consistent with Supply Chain Optimization</u>

People can clearly demonstrate how decisions are made in support of the formal supply chain objectives and optimization.

c. <u>Payment Terms</u>

Payment terms do not distort demand and supply patterns. The distortion that can occur due to payment terms is understood, and processes exist to negate the impact on the supply chain.

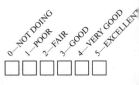

d. <u>Transfer Pricing</u>

Transfer pricing is used for treasury purposes and does not distort decision making by supply chain members.

19. Team-based supply chain activities are the norm. The team includes suppliers and customers.

a. <u>Extended Enterprise Teams</u>

Roles and responsibilities are clear and understood between trading partners. Business processes and enablers are clearly understood by relevant teams and individuals from the trading partners and drive team behaviors. Teams are made up of members from the extended enterprise, not just from our enterprise.

b. <u>Win-Win Relationships</u>

The culture and behaviors in the supply chain encourage partners to share improvements and costs to the total benefit of the supply chain.

c. <u>"Do What We Say We Will Do"</u>

There is a culture of "doing what we say we will do" in all interactions. Strategies and plans are accepted and owned between partners. The silence is approval concept is fully understood and used.

d. <u>Meetings with Formal Agenda</u>

Regular and effective reviews with formal agenda are held between key members of all the collaborative steps in the supply chain.

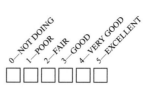

e. <u>Openness and Honesty</u>

Honesty and openness are hallmarks of all communications between all trading partners.

BUSINESS PERFORMANCE MEASURES

The expected suite of business performance measures will include the following core measures, supplemented by business specific measures dependent on strategy focus.

The standard for each measure will be either upper-quartile performance, a minimum standard of 99.5 percent, or attainment of business plan (as indicated). This measure demonstrates continuous performance improvement.

1. <u>Customer Service</u>
   On-time delivery to promise: On-Time-In-Full (OTIF) at every step.
   Measurement standard: Minimum standard
2. <u>Perfect Order</u>
   The concept of perfect order is understood and defined for the company.
   Measurement standard: Attainment of strategy
3. <u>Lead Time Performance</u>
   The length of time allowed in the planning system from the start to finish of a process. Each step and the entire extended supply chain are measured and reducing.
   Measurement standard: (a) Attainment of strategy; (b) upper-quartile performance
4. <u>Velocity Ratio</u>
   The added value time as a ratio of total elapsed time, for each step and for the entire extended supply chain, is measured and improving.
   Measurement standard: (a) Attainment of strategy; (b) upper-quartile performance.

5. Inventory Levels

   The value of inventory and the calculated inventory turns in the entire supply chain is measured and improving.

   Measurement standard: (a) Attainment of strategy; (b) upper-quartile performance

6. Total Delivered Cost

   The concept of Total Delivered Cost is understood and defined for the company.

   Measurement standard: Attainment of strategy

8

MANAGING INTERNAL SUPPLY

PURPOSE

To manage capabilities and resources to deliver the internal supply plan and to execute the business supply strategies through integrated supply planning and control to upper-quartile performance.

Chapter Content

Supply Strategy
Integration
Master Supply Planning
Material and Resource Planning
Executing the Schedule
Data Integrity
Acquisition and Effective Use and Care of Assets
Performance Measurement
Behavioral Characteristics
BUSINESS PERFORMANCE MEASURES

SUPPLY STRATEGY

1. The supply strategy supports the operations strategy and business strategy and drives supply planning and execution.

a. Alignment to Strategic Business Objectives

The role, purpose, and focus of the operating unit is defined and objectives have been set to optimize the supply chain. Each operating unit can demonstrate an understanding of how its role fits with the extended supply chain and the operations strategy. Priorities are clearly communicated, understood, and tracked.

b. Impact of Strategy is Understood

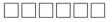

The trade-offs for delivering the operating unit's strategy have been identified, valued, and understood. Competing objectives throughout the supply chain have been identified and reconciled. Core competencies and capabilities are defined and there is a formal outsourcing strategy for noncore areas of the business.

c. Ability to Demonstrate Improvement

A long-term improvement plan takes into account the assessed maturity of current supply processes and determines gap-closing actions required to optimize business performance. Demonstrated capability and aggregate resource management techniques are used to ensure validity of the improvement plan.

2. A supply model exists and supports the operations strategy and states the key operational policies for the supply unit.

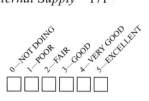

a. <u>Supply Objectives</u>

The operations strategy is derived from and supports the market strategy, which defines the required responsiveness, flexibility, and service levels. This drives the internal supply model, which includes plans to optimize customer service/satisfaction, inventory, quality, and costs.

b. <u>Response/Supply Model Definition</u>

The point at which we meet the customer is clearly understood. This drives supply strategies such as make to stock, make to order, and so on. Competitor capabilities and customer requirements are well understood and are prime inputs to the definition.

c. <u>Hedging for Flexibility</u>

Hedging policy is formally documented, evaluated, and approved by senior management. Policy is routinely reviewed to ensure alignment with changing conditions while maintaining consistency with the supply model. Reliance on hedging is being reduced by understanding the root causes and deploying improvement plans.

d. <u>Customer Satisfaction Focus</u>

There is an intense focus on improving customer satisfaction, which is monitored and reported widely.

e. <u>Process Teams</u>

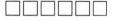

Partnerships and process teams collaborate in driving stated expectations and performance.

INTEGRATION

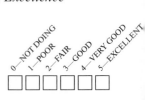

3. Internal supply capability and flexibility is modeled, measured, and managed through a monthly supply review process with supply chain and external sourcing. Integration with product management, demand, and financial planning is ensured through an Integrated Business Planning process.

a. <u>Process Mechanism</u>

The linkage between supply chain management and other elements in the Integrated Business Planning process is defined and made explicit.

b. <u>Linkage to Product Management and Demand</u>

Plans are received from Product Management and Demand as "requirements" to the monthly supply planning process. Integrated supply plans are created, recognizing capability and flexibility within the extended supply chain.

c. <u>Linkage within the Supply Chain</u>

Input is received from Internal Supply and External Sourcing identifying capability and flexibility. Plans developed for the extended supply chain direct planning for Internal Supply and External Sourcing.

d. <u>Linkage to Financial Planning</u>

Evaluated supply chain plans and assumptions provide visibility to financial planning on activity level, cost, inventory, and capital investment implications. The scope is the corporate supply chain and not just the parts, countries, or operating units. The financial planning process utilizes the latest supply chain plans including planned cost reduction and improvement actions.

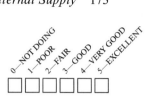

e. <u>Reconciliation Management</u>

Supply Chain Management is proactive in seeking business solutions where the proposed plan implies constraint on either product management or demand plans, gaps to business commitments, or where risks are deemed unacceptable. Adjustments made in Integrated Reconciliation or at the Management Business Review are incorporated within revised supply plans

4. Processes exist to forge the operating links required for day-to-day execution, providing visibility, control of uncertainty, and enabling consistent and improving performance to achieve Strategic Business Objectives.

a. <u>Scope of the Operating Unit</u>

The operating unit's role is clearly defined. Planning parameters are clear; they support the operations strategy and are consistently being challenged and improved. Supply assumptions are explicit and are reviewed at least monthly.

b. <u>Interface with the External Supply Chain</u>

Supply chain links have been mapped, and there is a high level of understanding of the steps, their purpose, and added value. Team-based partnerships and collaborative agreements exist with customers and suppliers.

c. <u>Interfacing within the Internal Supply Chain</u>

Processes for interfacing between steps in the supply chain are effective and enable change to be proactively and effectively managed, resulting in supply chain agility. Within these processes, problem resolution and performance reviews are clearly defined and improvements are being demonstrated.

d. Gaps Are Identified and Are Explicit

Gaps between the supply plan and strategic business objectives are visible and there are processes to reconcile their differences. Financially analyzed options and recommendations to close gaps are developed for senior management approval.

e. Processes Are Well Integrated

Business Excellence is understood and is used to drive improvements above the current level of performance. Processes delivering less than 99.5 percent performance are known and improvement plans are being deployed. Processes and systems are integrated across the supply chain and there is evidence that process knowledge is being captured in one database.

MASTER SUPPLY PLANNING

5. A master supply planning process exists to ensure completeness and management of internal supply.

a. The Supply Planner

The Supply Planner manages the plan to ensure that commitments to customers are met in full and to optimize both inventory and the efficiency of the business. The Supply Planner operates within current policies and is a major contributor to their improvement.

b. Plans

All demands are considered in the master supply plans, which drive all supporting supply plans. The master supply plan at an appropriate level of detail extends over the Integrated Business Planning horizon, allowing sufficient visibility to incorporate future requirements.

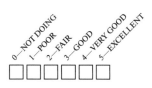

c. <u>Strategies and Tactics Creating Valid Plans</u>

There is an intense focus on creating and delivering valid plans that are aligned with strategies and derived from tactics. The plans are customer-focused, integrated, and utilize appropriate management and planning techniques.

d. <u>Rough-Cut Capacity Planning</u>

A formal process defines key resources and indicates their criticality to changing business conditions. Critical resources are managed and goals are set to optimize those resources, both internal and external.

e. <u>Systems, Tools, and Data</u>

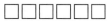

Required systems and tools are provided, fully understood, and operated by educated and trained people. These tools are fully integrated and can be operated at various levels of detail, over varying time frames. Employees routinely seek opportunities to improve the use of planning tools and techniques and are confident that data are accurate.

f. <u>Planning and Scheduling Techniques</u>

The planning process provides clear direction on appropriate planning and scheduling techniques and the setting up and use of key planning parameters and rules, all of which are clearly understood and formally applied. Decision support tools and advanced planning systems are applied where appropriate.

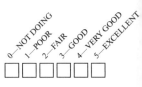

g. <u>Manage the Master Supply Schedule</u>

The master supply schedule is established to enable management by exception across the entire cumulative lead time and at the appropriate level of detail. Planners' activity is driven from system-generated action messages that are prioritized, reviewed, and resolved in a timely manner.

6. Capable people are managing all supply plans, including logistics planning.

a. <u>Planner Competence and Accountability</u>

Those responsible for planning and scheduling are educated and trained to operate at best-practice standards. They understand supply and material processes and systems and are held accountable for creating and maintaining valid plans to support business goals. Planners are responsible for creating, maintaining, reviewing, and analyzing the validity of planning parameters and rules.

b. <u>Managing Change with Time Fences</u>

Time Fences have been identified, recognized, and actively used to manage change. Supplier time fences are known and rules are recognized, to ensure that promises or changes are not made that cannot be honored. Processes are in place to actively reduce Lead Times and to align Time Fences with greater business agility.

c. <u>What-if Analysis and the Impact of Change</u>

Requests for change are modeled within the formal planning and scheduling system to determine their overall effect, such as their impact on customer service, all supply plans, and costs.

d. <u>Driving Improvements</u>

Those responsible for planning and scheduling understand performance measures and proactively use Root Cause Analysis to identify improvement opportunities. Challenging the status quo is common behavior, with documented improvements in many areas, such as reduced lead times, order quantities, and reduced reliance on safety buffers.

e. <u>Policies, Process, and Procedures</u>

Formal documentation addresses all policy, process, procedure, and work instruction requirements for supply planning and scheduling. The planning process is not reliant on key individuals whose absence may inhibit best practice and attaining excellent results.

MATERIAL AND RESOURCE PLANNING

7. There is a formal Material Requirements Planning process that is integrated with, and supports, the Master Supply Plan/ Schedule.

a. <u>Defined Process</u>

There is a detailed Material Requirements Planning process that maintains valid material plans, along with a control process that communicates priorities through production schedules, supplier schedules, or pull mechanisms.

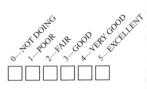

b. <u>Formal Priority-Setting Mechanism</u>

The only priority-setting mechanism is operated through the formal system, and is either date (schedule), sequence, or demand (pull) driven. All other informal, priority-setting mechanisms (shortage lists, hot lists, priority codes, and so on) have been eliminated. The planner is responsible for the priorities, using dates, sequence, or pull signals.

c. <u>Planning Activities Are Conducted Within the Integrated System</u>

A fully integrated system controls material and/ or resource plans, which are expressed in weekly, daily, or smaller time periods so as to enable identification of priorities and resolution of conflicts.

d. <u>Managing the Work Location Schedules</u>

Schedules are constantly updated to be meaningful to the operating environment. Planners understand the system capability and rules and are responsible for the resulting plan. No items in the materials plan are past due.

e. <u>Supplier Scheduling</u>

Supplier schedules are used to inform suppliers of firm and planned supply requirements. Based on agreed Time Fences and Lead Times. These requirements are communicated at least weekly, and more frequently if necessary.

8. There is a capability planning and scheduling process based on demonstrated capability that supports execution of the detailed supply schedule.

a. Level of Detail for Capability Planning

Capacity Requirements Planning (Capability Planning) is used with processes that depend on detailed routings. Validity for processes that do not require this level of control is maintained through rough cut capacity planning.

b. Capability Planning

A capacity planning process is used to ensure that requirements can be met at each Resource Center, within planned capacity by day. Resource Centers are properly defined to enable control of priorities and capacities while minimizing data maintenance, transactions, and reports. There is a formal weekly planning review, culminating in a weekly commitment to the short-term capacity needs.

c. Finite Scheduling

When a Finite Solver or equivalent is used the rules ensure that resulting schedules are realistic and are aligned with the master supply plan maintaining the integrity of customer promises.

d. Demonstrated Capacity

Demonstrated Capacity is measured and used to update planned capacity and is presented along with planned, maximum, and required capacity. A Load Factor is the preferred measure to communicate capability to the planning and scheduling system and to drive improvements. Components making up the Load Factor are understood and a process exists to gain improvement.

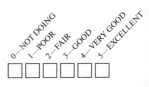

e. Improvement Culture

Time-phased improvement plans are deployed to increase demonstrated capacity by Resource Centers; there is evidence that operational efficiencies are being increased.

EXECUTING THE SCHEDULE

9. Processes exist to ensure that there is a commitment to execute the schedule.

a. Deliver the Schedule

Accountability is assigned to meet the schedule, which is refreshed at least daily. Production demonstrates a commitment to 99.5 percent schedule adherence and consistently achieves performance greater than 99.5 percent.

b. Effective Daily Review

There is a daily schedule review process where the current issues are resolved, queue levels are reviewed, and there is a recommitment to the schedule.

c. Documentation

The execution process is documented in work instructions that have been designed utilizing team input, and a formal change control process exists.

d. Supplier Scheduling

Where Supplier Schedules drive supplier deliveries performance is measured and achieves a minimum of 99.5 percent. Where pull techniques are used the number of Kanban violations is less than 0.5 percent.

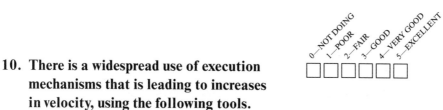

10. There is a widespread use of execution mechanisms that is leading to increases in velocity, using the following tools.

a. <u>Execution Communication</u>

Wherever possible, communication utilizes visual and audible mechanisms. There is a plan in place to visualize work execution processes.

b. <u>Kanban</u>

Demand-pull mechanisms are widely understood by suppliers and production, and where applicable are used to control flow of material. All Kanbans have specific operating rules, which are rigorously adhered to. There is evidence that the size and number of Kanbans is being challenged routinely to determine if they meet current or near-term business conditions and drive improvement.

c. <u>Velocity and Lot Size</u>

Velocity Ratio is measured and reported, and improvements are being made, resulting in reductions in lot sizes and lead times.

d. <u>Waste Elimination Culture and Behavior</u>

The elimination of waste from business processes is a stated objective and there is an active and visible program to empower people and teams to identify and eliminate waste. Balanced efficiency measures are used to improve supply chain performance.

e. Physical Material Management

Where material is located in an execution environment, those that operate in that environment are responsible for its management and control. Point-of-Use material control techniques are prevalent.

DATA INTEGRITY

11. Product and process data integrity is guaranteed through formal and timely creation, maintenance, and auditing of all data.

a. Master Data

The monthly audit is achieving accuracy at a minimum of 99.5 percent.

b. Bills of Material/Requirements (and Material Specifications)

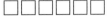

The monthly audit is recording accuracy at a minimum of 99.5 percent.

c. Routings

The monthly audit is recording accuracy at a minimum of 99.5 percent.

d. Rules

The monthly audit is recording accuracy at a minimum of 99.5 percent.

e. Work Location

The monthly audit is recording accuracy at a minimum of 99.5 percent.

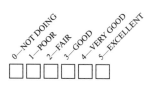

f. <u>Inventory Record Accuracy</u>

The monthly audit is recording accuracy at a minimum of 99.5 percent.

12. The integrity of dynamic data is maintained by timely and accurate transaction recording, including the capture of current capability information resulting from improvement initiatives.

a. <u>Transaction Integrity</u>

Any transaction recording is timely, accurate, and fully integrated within the planning and control system; appropriate tools are provided and the system reflects reality, with most data capture in real time. There is no duplicate data capture taking place.

b. <u>Lead Times</u>

Lead Time policies include intent to continually challenge and decrease lead times. All Lead Times are continually reviewed.

c. <u>Order Quantities</u>

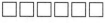

There is a process to determine the order quantity policy, which is consistent with the supply model. Kanban numbers and quantity are similarly managed. Order quantities are continually reviewed.

d. <u>Safety Stock</u>

There is a process for determining the optimum level of Safety Stock. If the supply model requires strategic Safety Stock, the executive owns this component.

e. <u>Improvement Plan</u>

Plans exist to reduce the number of transactions and/or eliminate errors. There are plans to minimize or eliminate the causes of Safety Stock and other safety parameters.

ACQUISITION AND EFFECTIVE USE AND CARE OF ASSETS

13. The company recognizes the value of its capital assets and cares for them, to ensure their sustained availability to add value and maximize their life.

a. <u>Acquisition</u>

Total Cost of Ownership is the basis for selecting new assets. Process capabilities and required flexibility are agreed on and defined. Full understanding of health, safety, and environmental risks and procedures is gained before the selection process is complete. Cash flow implications and change in capability are reflected in the Integrated Business Planning Process. Commissioning and process validation is compliant with all requirements.

b. <u>Breakdown Investigation</u>

Equipment and systems breakdown or uncertain reliability is rare. Root Cause Analysis is conducted to reduce and eliminate occurrences. Appropriate information is published to ensure management focus and action.

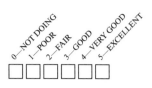

c. Planned Maintenance

Maintenance routines are derived from equipment manufacturer information and from experience, to ensure that the asset functions at its optimum level. Maintenance of equipment is planned into the master supply plan. There is an active and formal Total Productive Maintenance program implemented across the operating unit.

d. Predictive Maintenance

Condition monitoring is used to assess the condition of critical equipment, especially when there is no backup resource available. Maintenance and repair is timed so as to extend Mean Time Between Failure and to reduce Mean Time to Recover.

e. Availability

The availability of processes, plant, and equipment at the required time of use is a prime driver of maintenance activity and is a focus of Continuous Improvement. There is no unscheduled down time for normal-cause events.

14. The capability of physical processes is understood and people at all levels are trained and educated to ensure the most effective use of assets.

a. Safety

Best practice and personal protective equipment and asset safety features are in use at all times. Evidence and published measures show that the company works to be a good citizen and demonstrates that accidents and incidents are investigated and are reducing. Upper-quartile performance is expected.

b. <u>Asset Capability</u>

The capability of plant, equipment, and systems is understood. A process exists to communicate this capability to product management to ensure that it is taken into account when developing new products and/or services for the company's port-folio and technology and for manufacturability.

c. <u>Appropriate User Education</u>

Education and training is provided to everyone involved in the use of an asset, to improve un-derstanding, and to optimize its use in the busi-ness. This includes an understanding of the critical characteristics of the asset, their impact on the quality of products and asset longevity, proper operating techniques, and understanding of the asset's limitations.

d. <u>Housekeeping and Organization</u>

All work environments are orderly, clean, and lack clutter. Material flows in an optimum man-ner to minimize the number of touches and material movement. Housekeeping audits are performed routinely and workplace organiza-tion programs have become the norm.

e. <u>Optimized Use of Assets</u>

There are measures in place to evaluate the effect of the asset maintenance program, such as Load Factor and improved velocity. It is understood that these measures are to improve the overall demonstrated performance and expose Load Factor issues, not to undermine a valid schedule.

PERFORMANCE MEASUREMENT

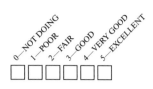

15. A balanced set of measures exists to manage and improve processes and performance related to managing internal supply. All measures have ownership and accountability and are integrated as part of a company suite to drive Business Improvement.

a. <u>Integrated Suite</u>

There is a visible path linking process measures to the overall business measures. All measures are designed to drive the desired behavior and performance. They are vertically and horizontally integrated and they are consistent across all internal supply processes. Measures are team based and include a balance of input, process, and output measures.

b. <u>Ownership and Accountability</u>

Performance measures are actively used and displayed for day-to-day control and to identify and drive improvement priorities. Employee understanding and acceptance of the methodology and reasoning behind each measure is high.

c. <u>Goal Driven by Strategic Business Objectives</u>

There is a benchmarking program to identify upper-quartile performance. There is a process to update measures to reflect changes in strategy, supply chain, and/or benchmarking activities. New measures are introduced with thorough analysis, communication, and documentation. Employees understand these measures and how they relate to Strategic Business Objectives.

d. <u>Targets and Tolerances</u>

Supply management uses targets and tolerances to set objectives based on benchmark data; there is evidence that targets and tolerances are continually revised. Management aspires to achieve these targets.

e. <u>Work Life Balance</u>

Measures include stakeholder satisfaction, job satisfaction, capability improvements, and quality of work life. The Team Leader uses this information for improvement initiatives. Internal gateway performance is improving.

16. There is a formal process for data collection, analysis, and reporting that covers the entire operating unit.

a. <u>Definitions and Calculations</u>

Definitions and calculations are held in a central repository and are widely accessible. Ownership, method of calculation, purpose, change control, and so forth are formally maintained and current.

b. <u>Collection, Publication, and Communication</u>

There is a formal process that delivers accurate and timely information; the process includes a routine review of measures for relevance, tolerances, targets, source data integrity, and calculations. There are standard reporting formats, simple (visual) presentations, and the publication is timely and coordinated.

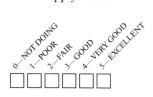

c. Root Cause Analysis and Corrective Action

Root Cause Analysis uses simple techniques such as histograms, Pareto charts, and Scatter Diagrams, and so on, and they are clearly posted and visible for all to learn from. Corrective action plans are always developed and executed to improve out-of-tolerance measures as well as all misses.

BEHAVIORAL CHARACTERISTICS

17. Behaviors support the meeting of customer expectations through the optimization of internal supply processes. Desired behavioral characteristics that are consistent with the operating strategy have been clearly defined and communicated.

a. Education and Training

All employees understand their role in meeting operational targets. The relevant education and training has been provided to ensure that employees understand and support the processes. There is a multiskilled workforce in place, valued and continually being developed.

b. Team-Based Activity

Multifunctional team activity, focused on operational targets, is well established. High-performance teams and Continuous Improvement programs have been fully adopted. Teams are recognized for their quantitative/tangible as well as qualitative/intangible achievements.

c. <u>No Artificial Pushes</u>

There are no artificial pushes (e.g., end of the day/week/month crunch). Smooth flow has been established and aligns with expectations.

d. <u>Visual Work Environment</u>

There is a desire to simplify the work environment to promote safety, throughput, and reduction of cost. People value their work space and keep it clean, uncluttered, and well organized.

e. <u>Supply Chain Processes</u>

Process-based thinking has become a way of life. Supply chain thinking predominates, and processes transcend functions to optimize the whole—not the parts.

f. <u>Customer-Centric</u>

There is a passion for customers' success, based on an understanding of their requirements.

18. There is trust in the numbers that make up the plans, and in people's ability to execute these plans.

a. <u>Trust and Facts</u>

There is a common, agreed, and shared master supply plan within the company. Complete trust in the quality of this plan can be demonstrated by every function. There is evidence that decisions are fact based and data driven, and are focused on optimizing the delivery of the supply plan.

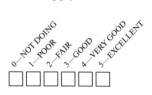

b. <u>Belief in Behavior</u>

The supply team believe in realistic and honest plans, as well as being proactive and flexible in responding to changes. Unnecessary levels in planning and execution have been identified and eliminated to facilitate improved communication.

c. <u>Work the Supply Plan</u>

There is a culture of planning the work and working to the plan.

d. <u>Silence Is Approval</u>

All those involved in the internal supply processes operate on the principle of communicating anticipated issues early, and that in the absence of issues and communications, silence means approval.

BUSINESS PERFORMANCE MEASURES

The expected suite of business performance measures will include the following core measures, supplemented by business-specific measures that are dependent on strategy focus.

The standard for each measure will be either upper-quartile performance, a minimum standard of 99.5 percent, or attainment of business plan (as indicated). This measure demonstrates continuous performance improvement.

1. <u>Customer Service</u>
   On time deliver to promise: On-Time-In-Full (OTIF).
   Measurement standard: Minimum standard
2. <u>Aggregate Supply-Plan Performance</u>
   Achievement of the supply plan approved through the Integrated
   Business Planning process.
   Measurement standard: Plan attainment

3. Quality

Product defects are measured in parts per million and performance is improving.

Measurement standard: Minimum standard

4. Inventory Levels

The value of inventory or the calculated inventory turns in this operating unit is measured and improving.

Measurement standard: (a) Attainment of strategy; (b) upper-quartile performance

5. Lead-Time Performance

The length of time allowed in the planning system from start to finish of the internal supply process is measured and reducing.

Measurement standard: (a) Attainment of strategy; (b) upper-quartile performance

6. Velocity

The added value time as a ratio of total elapsed time for internal supply is measured and improving.

Measurement standard: (a) Attainment of strategy; (b) upper-quartile performance

9

MANAGING EXTERNAL SOURCING

PURPOSE

To source and manage the incoming supply of goods and services to competitive advantage, ensuring upper-quartile supply chain performance. To understand and manage the balance between risk and total cost of ownership.

Chapter Content

External and Internal Sourcing Strategies (Activities, Materials, Services, and so on)
Integration with Strategy and Business Planning Process
External Sourcing Strategy
Total Cost of Ownership
Continuity of Supply
Supplier Analysis and Selection and Business Agreements
Supplier Relationships
Behavioral Characteristics
Performance Measurement
BUSINESS PERFORMANCE MEASURES

EXTERNAL AND INTERNAL SOURCING STRATEGIES (ACTIVITIES, MATERIALS, SERVICES, AND SO ON)

1. **The external and internal sourcing strategy is derived from the company's Operations Strategy and is reflected in the procurement activities.**

   a. <u>Documented Strategy</u>

   A sourcing strategy exists that defines those items or services that, for strategic reasons, the company has defined to be internally sourced. For all other items or services, potential external sources of supply are evaluated together with internal sourcing options.

   b. <u>Review Process</u>

   The external and internal sourcing strategy is documented and reviewed regularly to ensure that it is congruent with the overall business strategy and that it meets current business needs.

   c. <u>Strategy Development</u>

   The development of the external and internal sourcing strategy is a cross-functional activity, with Procurement participation.

   d. <u>Comparison of Benefits</u>

   A process exists for the valid comparison of costs and benefits between internal and external sources of supply, using a Total Cost of Ownership template for all significant requirements.

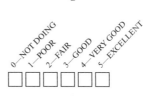

2. The business recognizes the key role of Procurement in prioritizing resources for those activities that provide the highest value add benefit and are aligned with the future development of the business.

a. <u>Innovation</u>

There is clear accountability for the Procurement function to proactively seek new core competencies at external sources of supply.

b. <u>Core Competencies</u>

The potential strategic benefits of new core competencies within the supplier base are fully evaluated in the external and internal sourcing decision-making process.

c. <u>Make/Buy Decisions</u>

The cross-functional process for the make/buy decision includes an understanding of potential consequences to the supplier base. If sourced internally these consequences are managed effectively. It fully evaluates all internal or external investment requirements.

d. <u>Review Process</u>

The actual costs and benefits of the make/buy decision are calculated and measured against the original estimates, to gauge how successful the decision-making process has been and to learn for the future.

INTEGRATION WITH STRATEGY AND BUSINESS PLANNING PROCESSES

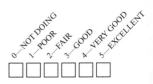

3. **External supply capability and flexibility is modeled, measured, and managed through the monthly Supply Review process with supply chain and internal supply. Integration with Product Management Review, Demand Review, and the financials is ensured through the Integrated Business Planning process.**

a. <u>Process Mechanism</u>

The linkage between external supply and the other process elements in Integrated Business Planning is defined and made explicit, irrespective of whether this is an integrated business unit or a stand-alone activity in a multientity organization.

b. <u>Linkage to Product Management</u>

Plans received from Product Management for the introduction of new and modified products and services, and product and service discontinuation, take full account of supplier capabilities and commitments made. This includes the implications of integrating new core competencies within the supplier base.

c. <u>Linkage to Supply Chain Management</u>

The head of Procurement is in attendance at the Supply Review and is accountable for ensuring that external sourcing plans are consistent with monthly supply chain plans.

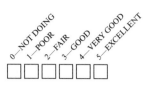

d. <u>Linkage to Financial Planning</u>

Evaluated external sourcing plans and assumptions provide visibility to financial planning of activity, cost, and investment implications. The financial planning process utilizes the latest external sourcing plans, including planned cost reduction and improvement actions.

e. <u>Reconciliation Management</u>

Procurement is proactive in seeking business solutions where the proposed plan implies constraint on Product Management or supply chain plans, gaps to business commitments, or where risks are unacceptable. Adjustments made in Integrated Reconciliation or at the Management Business Review are incorporated within revised external sourcing plans.

4. Suppliers' capability in terms of capacity, quality, and technological support are analyzed in developing and agreeing to the Master Supply Plan.

a. <u>Supply Planning</u>

Suppliers' key resource capacity and potential constraints are understood and regularly reviewed. There is a process for identifying potential capacity constraints within the supplier base.

b. <u>Supplier Initiatives</u>

Key supplier initiatives affecting their capability are formally reviewed as part of the Supply Review step of the Integrated Business Planning process.

c. <u>Supplier Quality</u>

Supplier quality processes and improvement programs are monitored and reported, to ensure integration with the company's quality systems.

d. <u>Technological Support</u>

There is a process to ensure that suppliers' technological capability matches the company's proposed future product portfolio plan.

EXTERNAL SOURCING STRATEGY

5. The external sourcing strategy supports the Operations Strategy and drives Procurement activities.

a. <u>Company Values</u>

The company's sourcing strategies and activities fully incorporate the company values. These are well understood by the Procurement team.

b. <u>Review Process</u>

There is a formal review of the documented external sourcing strategy, to ensure alignment with the company's Value Proposition and strategy.

c. <u>*e*-Procurement Strategy</u>

The company has a clearly defined *e*-procurement strategy that differentiates between the transactional benefits to be gained and the longer term strategic goals of *e*-sourcing. This is based on the commodity group profile.

d. <u>Alternative Supply Channels</u>

The company continually evaluates opportunities with alternative sources of supply, taking into account such factors as geography, industry, and regulatory, to create competitive advantage.

6. Externally sourced materials and services are grouped together into logical groups such as commodities, categories, and so on, and a clear sourcing strategy is defined for each group.

a. <u>Commodity Groupings</u>

Commodity groupings have been agreed and documented.

b. <u>Commodity Group Allocation</u>

All externally sourced materials and services (including intracompany where appropriate) have been allocated a commodity group.

c. <u>Commodity Group Profiling</u>

Commodity group profiling is carried out on a regular basis, taking into account factors such as cost, risk, technology, vulnerability, and strategic significance.

d. <u>Commodity Group Acquisition Strategy</u>

For each commodity group, the planned and most appropriate approach for acquisition, considering quality, service, capacity, and total cost of ownership, is considered.

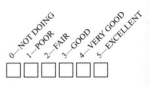

e. Single/Multisourcing

A formal Risk Analysis is carried out for those materials and services where supply availability is considered to be vulnerable. Single and/or multisourcing policies are aligned to this.

TOTAL COST OF OWNERSHIP

7. Total Cost of Ownership is recognized to be the decision-making tool for assessing competing suppliers in making sourcing decisions.

a. Assessment

Total Cost of Ownership is recognized as the key tool in the strategic sourcing process.

b. Procurement Measurement

Total Cost Ownership is used as the key tool to measure the effectiveness of Procurement.

c. Traditional Measures

Traditional performance measures such as purchase price variance have been replaced by Total Cost of Ownership.

d. Cross-Functional Participation

The Total Cost Ownership template for each commodity group has been agreed by all appropriate functions, including finance.

8. A Total Cost of Ownership analysis is in place to consistently calculate lifetime costs for all key materials, goods, and services.

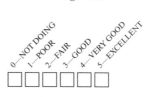

a. <u>Template</u>

The Total Cost of Ownership template takes into account the present value of all costs that will be incurred over the expected life of the product or service.

b. <u>Inclusion of All Costs</u>

The template includes all aspects of the total cost, including price, and factors such as transport costs, quality costs, on time delivery performance, inventory holding, response times from the supplier, projected exchange rate fluctuations, processing costs, servicing and maintenance costs, resale value, and disposal costs.

c. <u>Commodity Group Profiling</u>

The Total Cost Ownership template is developed for each commodity grouping used in commodity group profiling.

d. <u>Periodic Reviews</u>

Total Cost Ownership templates are reviewed regularly to ensure validity. Changes in key variables, such as currency exchange rates and interest rates, are captured.

e. <u>Interim and Final Reviews</u>

Periodically, and at the end of the lifetime of the material or service purchased, the actual total cost is compared to the projected total cost at the time of the original calculation. This comparison is used to aid future learning.

CONTINUITY OF SUPPLY

9. The complete supply chain for all strategically significant, externally sourced materials and services is fully documented.

a. <u>Documentation</u>

The supply chain for all strategically significant products and services is mapped; constraints, risks, and contingency measures are identified.

b. <u>First-Tier Suppliers</u>

The responsibilities of first-tier suppliers in terms of the management of their own supplier base are properly defined.

c. <u>Second- and Third-Tier Suppliers</u>

Where appropriate, second- and third-tier suppliers are reviewed for long-term capability in the same way as first-tier suppliers.

d. <u>End Use and Consumption</u>

Future changes in end use markets are understood and documented to evaluate vulnerabilities and opportunities to the incoming supply chain.

10. Analysis methods are used to minimize risk to the company by ensuring the continuity of externally sourced materials and services.

a. <u>Risk Analysis</u>

Regular risk studies are carried out on all key suppliers, using appropriate analysis tools.

b. <u>Supplier Financial and Business Performance</u>

There is a process to review key financial ratios and business performance indicators for all major suppliers and strategically significant second- and third-tier suppliers.

c. Supplier Internal Systems

Suppliers' internal processes and systems are reviewed to ensure that they are sufficient to support the requirements of the company's business.

d. Disaster Recovery Planning

There is a disaster recovery plan in place for all commodities and suppliers where the company is vulnerable. These plans are regularly reviewed and updated.

SUPPLIER ANALYSIS AND SELECTION AND BUSINESS AGREEMENTS

11. There is a structured supplier evaluation and selection process for each commodity that takes into account all the relevant requirements for that commodity.

a. Cross-Functional Involvement

The evaluation and selection of suppliers is considered to be a cross-functional activity, facilitated by the Procurement function.

b. Breadth of Process

The process takes into account, where appropriate, manufacturing processes, quality systems, service support, Health, Safety, and Environment, new product development activities, and all other relevant business processes. It also ensures that sourcing with the proposed supplier would not compromise the company's values.

c. <u>Financial Viability</u>

Supplier financial viability is considered as part of the selection process.

d. <u>Parent Company Relationship</u>

Where the supplier is part of a larger group, the parent company's relationship in terms of meeting requirements, ensuring continuity of supply, and so on, is taken into account. The supplier's strategic significance to the parent company is also evaluated.

e. <u>Capacity Constraints</u>

Supplier key capacity constraints are understood and taken into account and managed in Master Supply Planning.

f. <u>Transparency of Decision Making</u>

The reasons for supplier selection are fully understood and documented.

12. In addition to the company's standard terms and conditions, Business Agreements are drawn up and exchanged with key suppliers, as appropriate to the nature of the supply.

a. <u>Business Agreement Structure</u>

The Business Agreement describes the way that the two companies will conduct the business between them, and include items such as expected standards of behavior and ethics, communication channels, time fences, flexibility of supply, review processes, joint projects, and technological support.

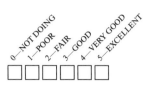

b. <u>Performance Levels</u>

The Business Agreement will specify agreed performance levels and measures and continuous improvement activities agreed between the company and the supplier.

c. <u>New Suppliers</u>

For new suppliers, there is a clear process for communicating the company's organization, job roles, business processes, and values.

d. <u>Review Process</u>

There is an agreed review process in place for the Business Agreement itself, and the review takes place at least annually.

SUPPLIER RELATIONSHIPS

13. The company is committed to a supplier development program to sustain long-term business improvement objectives.

a. <u>Transfer of Information and Data</u>

There is a process in place to ensure the two-way transfer of collaborative demand and supply data and other information between the company and its suppliers. This process is as fast and flexible as necessary to meet the responsiveness required by the company's operating strategy. There are agreed rules in place to manage changes to data.

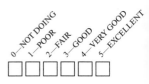

b. *e*-Procurement

e-procurement implementation takes into account current and planned *e*-technology developments both internally and within the supplier base. This understanding is integrated into the company's IT strategy.

c. Data Integrity

There is a measurement and review process in place to ensure that data shared with suppliers are timely and of high integrity and accuracy, and that the supplier master file data integrity achieves at least a minimum standard of 99.5 percent accuracy.

d. Waste Elimination

Joint programs with key suppliers are in place to identify and eliminate waste in the supply chain, using Root Cause Analysis and problem-solving tools. The Velocity Ratio is recognized as a key driver for joint process acceleration programs with appropriate suppliers.

e. Environmental Impact

Joint programs are in place with suppliers to improve environmental conditions over the complete product life cycle, including disposal and recycling of material.

f. Resource Allocation

Where joint improvement programs with suppliers require resources and/or people, the company has budgeted to make the required internal resources available.

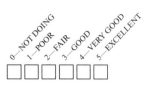

14. Suppliers are fully integrated into the company's Product Management process.

a. <u>Approved Sourcing List</u>

An approved sourcing list exists for priority commodity groups. This list has been agreed by Product Management and Procurement, and is reviewed at appropriate intervals.

b. <u>Procurement and Product Management Interface</u>

The cross-functional Product and Service Management team defines the point at which Procurement becomes involved in this process.

c. <u>Procurement and Supplier Involvement in Ideas and Technology</u>

Procurement and supplier involvement may include involvement at the concept design stage; membership of Product and Service Management teams; *e*-integration into the company's design systems; materials handling or packaging solutions.

d. <u>Supplier Product Development Role</u>

In some circumstances, the supplier may take a full partnership role, with responsibility for developing and supplying technology and complete products and services.

BEHAVIORAL CHARACTERISTICS

15. There is a clear statement of the ethical standards set by the company in dealing with its suppliers, and of the standards expected of the suppliers themselves.

a. <u>Supplier Review Process</u>

These ethical standards are included as part of the regular supplier review process and are provided to new suppliers.

b. <u>Suppliers' Internal Processes and Culture</u>

The ways in which the supplier communicates with and develops its own employees is reviewed and taken into account in the sourcing decision.

c. <u>Safety, Health, and Environment</u>

The company makes clear to the supplier its expectation that appropriate and effective Safety, Health, and Environmental standards are in place at the supplier.

d. <u>Supplier Behavioral Expectations</u>

The behavioral standards expected of suppliers are made clear, and processes are in place to ensure that the values and guiding standards in place at suppliers are consistent with the company's own.

16. The behavioral characteristics required from those who interface with external suppliers are defined with regard to the business relationships appropriate to those suppliers.

a. <u>Consistent Behaviors</u>

The overall supplier management tactics may be different between commodity groups, but the standards of ethics and behaviors are consistent once the commitment is made.

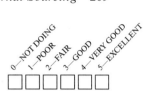

b. <u>Skills and Aptitudes of People</u>

The skills and aptitudes of all people involved are taken into account in determining their best fit for particular sourcing strategies.

c. <u>Training and Education</u>

Education is a key priority. Training is given as appropriate and is documented.

d. <u>"Do What You Say You Will Do"</u>

There is a culture of doing what you say you will do in all interactions. Strategies and plans are accepted and owned between partners. The Silence Is Approval concept is fully understood and shared.

PERFORMANCE MEASUREMENT

17. **A balanced set of measures exists to manage and improve processes and supplier performance in managing external sourcing. All measures have ownership and accountability and are integrated as part of a company suite to drive business improvement.**

a. <u>Supplier Delivery Performance</u>

Supplier delivery performance is measured, and both internal and external improvement actions are agreed.

b. <u>Improvement Metrics</u>

The suite of improvement metrics—including aspects such as quality performance, documentation accuracy, velocity, safety stock levels, order quantities, lead times, and delivery frequency—is defined, measured, and communicated—internally and externally.

c. <u>Quality Assurance</u>

Quality assurance standards, goals, and objectives are jointly agreed between the company and its suppliers—and documented. The methods of product quality verification, whether on-site or by certification, are defined and agreed.

d. <u>Technical Support Capability</u>

The supplier's capability in terms of technical support to product and service development or improvement is considered, as appropriate to the commodity group.

BUSINESS PERFORMANCE MEASURES

The expected suite of business performance measures will include the following core measures, supplemented by business-specific measures dependent on strategy and value proposition focus.

The standard for each measure will be either upper-quartile performance, a minimum standard of 99.5 percent, or attainment of business plan (as indicated). This measure demonstrates continuous performance improvement.

1. <u>Supplier Perfect Delivery</u>
   Availability on time, fit for purpose, to the correct location, with correct paperwork is measured and is improving.
   Measurement standard: Minimum standard

2. Quality

   Supplier quality is monitored appropriate to the relevant commodity group, is measured in parts per million (where possible),
   and is improving.

   Measurement standard: Minimum standard

3. Supplier Lead Time

   Replenishment time from demand signal to availability for use is
   measured and is decreasing.

   Measurement standard: upper-quartile performance

4. Supplier Lead Times for New Product Introduction

   Time to introduce new products or services from gate release to
   availability.

   Measurement standard: Plan attainment

5. Total Cost of Ownership Trend

   The total cost of ownership is being driven down.

   Measurement standard: Attainment of strategy

6. Inventory

   Purchased inventory, including consignment stock, by supplier, is
   measured and is aligned with strategic objectives.

   Measurement standard: upper-quartile performance

7. Velocity

   The added value time as a ratio of total elapsed time for externally
   sourced supply is measured and is improving.

   Measurement standard: (a) Attainment of strategy; (b) upper-
   quartile performance.

OLIVER WIGHT BIOGRAPHY

Oliver Wight was a pioneer in manufacturing. Ollie recognized the problems faced by manufacturing companies and had a clear understanding of their needs. He was always looking to the future and finding ways to improve things.

Oliver Wight had two great gifts. He could take complicated subjects, unravel them, and make them simple. More important, he had a sensitivity to people that broke down barriers. He had innovative ideas and was able to communicate them in a way that gained acceptance, commitment, and enthusiasm.

Somehow, in the early years of the computer revolution, the role of people was misplaced. Ollie made it his personal mission to put people back where they belong and to give them the understanding they need to use their new tools. Among his many enduring tenets is, "Computers are not the key to success, people are." This remains a core philosophy of The Oliver Wight Companies.

Oliver Wight used his gifts to build an enduring legacy in manufacturing. Nearly every company using ERP or MRP II and getting big increases in productivity, inventory turnover, and customer service had some association with Ollie, either through his Top Management courses, writing, or the verbal pass-along of his ideas, philosophies, and memorable one-liners. Ollie wrote four books and produced a series of videos that were widely used in manufacturing. His emphasis on the people side of manufacturing solutions earned him a reputation as a leading thinker in Business Education.

Ollie once said, quite modestly, "I've left some footprints." Those who have chosen to follow them are better off—both personally and professionally.

Oliver Wight was 53 years old when he passed away in 1983.